SEXUAL AVERSION, SEXUAL PHOBIAS, and PANIC DISORDER

Also by Helen Singer Kaplan, M.D., Ph.D.

The New Sex Therapy: Active Treatment of Sexual Dysfunction (1974, 1981)

Disorders of Sexual Desire (1979)

The Evaluation of Sexual Disorders: Psychological and Medical Aspects (with M. Horwith, M.D., J. Imperato-McGinley, M.D., S.A. Kaufman, M.D., E. Leiter, M.D., A. Melman, M.D., & J.M. Reckler, M.D.) (1983)

SEXUAL AVERSION, SEXUAL PHOBIAS,

and

PANIC DISORDER

by

Helen Singer Kaplan, M.D., Ph.D.

with a chapter by
Donald F. Klein, M.D.

BRUNNER/MAZEL *Publishers* • New York

Library of Congress Cataloging-in-Publication Data
Kaplan, Helen Singer
  Sexual aversion, sexual phobias, and panic disorder.
  Bibliography: pp. 151-154.
  Includes index.
  1. Sexual aversion disorders. 2. Panic disorders.
I. Klein, Donald F., 1928-   . II. Title.
[DNLM: 1. Anxiety Disorders—therapy. 2. Psychosexual
Disorders—therapy. WM 611 K17s]
RC560.S45K37 1987 616.85′83   86-28331
ISBN 0-87630-450-1

Copyright © 1987 by Helen Singer Kaplan, M.D., Ph.D.

Published by
BRUNNER/MAZEL, INC.
19 Union Square
New York, New York 10003

MANUFACTURED IN THE UNITED STATES OF AMERICA

to
Carroll and Milton Petrie

Contents

Chapter 1. Introduction: Sexual Panic States   3

Chapter 2. Clinical Features: The Sexual Avoidance Syndromes
and Panic Disorder   10

Chapter 3. Etiology: A Pluralistic Concept   37

Chapter 4. Sexual Disorders and Medication
by Donald F. Klein M.D.   68

Chapter 5. Treatment: An Integrated Approach   84

Chapter 6. The Couple with Sexual Panic Disorder:
Separation Anxiety and Conjoint Sex Therapy   125

Chapter 7. Drugs and the Psychodynamic Process:
Some Hypotheses and Speculations   139

Bibliography   151

Index   155

SEXUAL AVERSION, SEXUAL PHOBIAS, *and* PANIC DISORDER

CHAPTER 1

Introduction:
Sexual Panic States

The phobic avoidance of sex and sexual aversion disorders are the primary complaints of many patients who seek help for their sexual difficulties (Crenshaw, 1985). But despite their high prevalence, sexual panic states have received surprisingly little professional attention, and students in the field are hard put to find literature on this topic. Thus, sexual phobias have been specifically excluded from the category of phobic disorders in DSM-III (1980) and these syndromes have received no mention at all in the section on psychosexual disorders.

Recently, however, there has been growing interest in sexual panic states, and the American Psychiatric Association committee on psychosexual dysfunctions has recommended the addition of the new diagnostic entity *Sexual Aversion Disorders* which is to be subsumed under the larger category of *Disorders of Sexual Desire* in DSM-III-R. In our experience this is a valid clinical entity which merits the attention of sex therapists, and this book is devoted to these long neglected syndromes.

The second objective of this volume is to consider the implications of the high coincidence of panic disorder and sexual phobias and aversions which we have observed in our patients. These dual syndromes have provided an excellent vantage for studying the fascinating interplay between a presumably biological vulnerability to panic and the impact of cultural, neurotic and relationship stressors. In addition, we found that our sexually phobic patients with underlying panic disorders were often too anxious and panicky to benefit from sex therapy. For this reason we have been using medication known to block panics with these patients, and our experience with the combined use of antipanic drugs

3

and psychodynamically oriented sexual therapy gave us the opportunity to integrate biological and psychodynamic concepts of sexual anxiety and to develop comprehensive treatment strategies which are also described in this book.

PANIC DISORDER

Panic Disorder is a relatively new diagnostic category which comprises a group of anxious phobic patients with panic attacks who are not amenable to psychological treatments or to major or minor tranquilizers, but who have an excellent response to tricyclic antidepressant drugs.

Donald Klein, who first described this syndrome, has postulated that the anxiety experienced by patients with panic disorder is qualitatively different from that of neurotic individuals, and involves a pathologically sensitive CNS anxiety-regulating mechanism. According to this theory, this biological abnormality predisposes these individuals to spontaneous panic attacks, phobias, excessive separation anxiety, and the development of detrimental avoidance behaviors (Klein, 1964, Klein, 1980). Klein's finding that tricyclic antidepressant drugs (TCA) block the panic attacks of patients with panic disorders has been confirmed by numerous investigators, and other types of antidepressants, including drugs in the monoamine inhibiting (MAOI) category, have been found to have similar antipanic effects. This discovery constitutes a major breakthrough which has considerably improved the prognosis for patients with panic disorders, and these medications are now considered the treatment of choice for this syndrome.

The first time I recognized a patient with both panic disorder and sexual dysfunction was in 1976 at the human sexuality program of the Payne Whitney Clinic of the New York Hospital-Cornell Medical Center.*

Case Vignette #1: Rosa and Richard

Rosa was a 25-year-old woman who had been married to her 27-year-old husband for four years. The couple had known each other since high school and their relationship, apart from their sexual difficulty, was loving and close. The patient had no desire for sex and avoided all physical contact with her husband; in recent years she had developed an intense aversion to any physical intimacy with him. It was of special interest that this patient had

---

* This case was briefly described elsewhere (Kaplan, Fyer, & Novick, 1982).

failed to improve both with individual psychodynamically oriented psychotherapy and also with behaviorally oriented sex therapy. Rosa reported that two years of twice weekly psychotherapy had been beneficial in improving her depressed mood, but did not relieve her sexual difficulties, while the behaviorally oriented sex therapy program, which she and her husband had attended once a week for four months, actually aggravated her sexual fears and avoidance.

The patient's stated complaint was an absence of sexual desire (ISD) and sexual aversion, but the evaluation revealed that her low level of sexual interest was secondary to a phobic avoidance of sex. Her complaint was specific to sex with a partner and she was capable of having orgasms when masturbating by herself and immersed in sexual fantasy. However, Rosa had never been able to experience erotic sensations or arousal with her husband, who had been her only sexual partner. On several occasions, she had panicked when he had tried to make love to her and she had developed profound anticipatory anxiety and avoidance as well as, in the last four years, an increasing aversion to any situation that even remotely suggested sex.

In addition to her long-standing sexual complaint, this patient met the diagnostic criteria for panic disorder. She reported having experienced spontaneous panic attacks during her youth. She had also suffered from several transient phobias, had difficulties with separation, and had failed to respond to psychological therapies. Rosa's underlying panic disorder had never been diagnosed, nor had she been treated with appropriate medication in any of her prior therapeutic experiences.

This patient responded to a course of psychodynamically oriented therapy which was combined with tricyclic medication (Imipramine 75 mg.), with a complete remission of her sexual symptoms in 30 weekly sessions. On follow-up four years later, the patient, who had not taken medication since termination of treatment, reported that she and her husband had continued to enjoy frequent and mutually gratifying sexual relations. The couple had also had a child during this period.

MEDICATION AND THE PROCESS OF SEX THERAPY

Once we became aware of the possible coexistence of sexual dysfunction and panic disorder, it became apparent that this case was by no means unique or even uncommon.

We found that 25 percent of our patients with sexual phobias and aversions also met the criteria for panic disorder, which is significantly greater than 2 percent, the estimated prevalence of this syndrome in the general population (DSM-III, 1980) (see Table 1).

In retrospect, this should not have been surprising. Individuals with phobic anxiety syndrome, which was Klein's (1964) original term for panic disorder, are at high risk for developing phobic avoidances of all kinds. There was no reason to believe that sex would be an exception.

It also turned out that patients with these combined syndromes accounted for a number of puzzling treatment failures.

In our programs,* most patients with sexual phobias and aversions receive psychodynamically oriented sex therapy. This method combines therapeutically controlled exposures to the feared sexual situation to extinguish the patient's irrational fear of sex with brief psychodynamically oriented therapy to provide insight into deeper conflicts. Sexually phobic and aversive patients who have a normal capacity for anxiety ordinarily show an excellent response to this approach. However, patients with underlying panic disorder find treatment stressful and they tend to resist. They generally do not experience the expected desensitization effect, nor does insight into their underlying neurotic conflicts seem to facilitate their progress. Their fears are simply too intense. Instead of bringing improvement, sex therapy may actually aggravate their sexual panics and intensify their compelling urge to avoid sex.

For the last five years we have been using antipanic medication together with sex therapy on a regular basis for patients with sexual complaints and panic disorders. We have found that these drugs can protect the patient from panic attacks during the treatment process

TABLE 1

Prevalence of Panic Disorder in Patients with Sexual Avoidance†

	With Panic		Without Panic	
Phobic avoiders (N = 106)	26	25%	80	75%
Quiet avoiders (N = 267)	9	3%	258	97%
All patients who avoid sex (N = 373)	35	9%	338	91%

† These patients were evaluated in our programs between 1976 and 1986.
Sig. <.001

* These patients were seen at the Human Sexuality Program of the Payne Whitney Clinic and at our private center for the evaluation and treatment of sexual disorders.

and frequently make it possible for them to cooperate with and benefit from sex therapy.

It was not our purpose to prove that antidepressant medication is indicated for sexual panic states. The efficacy of the tricyclic antidepressants (TCDs), monoamine oxidase inhibitors (MAOIs) and alprazolam in the treatment of panic disorders has been well documented, and we did not feel it necessary to conduct additional controlled double-blind studies on the effects of these drugs on our population.

The use of medications that were known to block panic attacks in conjunction with sex therapy for patients who have both diagnoses was simply an application of this proven therapeutic modality to the area of sexuality in our attempt to provide more effective treatment for these difficult patients.

For many years, there had been a sharp split between behavioral and psychodynamically oriented clinicians about the causes and treatment of psychosexual disorders. But shortly after the integrated sex therapy methods were introduced in the 70s, it became clear that behavioral and dynamic methods actually complement and enhance each other. The combined approach came to be regarded as a major breakthrough, and the old fallacious controversy was laid to rest.

A comparable and equally false dichotomy has historically existed between psychological and biological psychiatry. The controversy has now diminished in the area of the psychoses, and today there is general consensus among health professionals that medication is indicated and beneficial for patients with schizophrenic psychoses and major affective disorders. However, the medication versus psychotherapy controversy is still very much alive with regard to anxiety, which has long been considered the province of the psychotherapist.

One source of these pointless arguments is that clinicians trained in psychopharmacology and those with psychological orientations do not understand each other's language and find it difficult to communicate. Scientifically minded psychopharmacologists are committed to relieving their patients' painful symptoms as rapidly and directly as possible. They are not, as a rule, interested in psychodynamics, nor in the subtle emotional nuances of the patients' experiences, which they regard as immaterial to their recovery. Psychiatrists with biological orientations tend to dismiss the accumulated wisdom of psychoanalysis as unscientific and of no proven benefit to patients, mainly, I think, because few have taken the trouble to study these theories in depth.

On the other hand, sensitive and humanistic analysts and therapists focus on the patient's feelings and inner experiences. They regard the quality of the therapeutic relationship as a crucial element for the success of treatment. Many of these dynamically oriented clinicians have no use for the biological approaches, and are critical of what they consider mechanical and manipulative solutions to human problems. Their failure to appreciate the potential benefits of psychoactive drugs is generally the result of their lack of understanding of the biological aspects of human behavior and their erroneous beliefs about the harmful effects of the new medications.

Since we started in 1970, we have worked with more than 2,000 patients and couples with sexual dysfunctions at the Human Sexuality Clinic at Payne Whitney and at our private center for the evaluation and treatment of sexual disorders in Manhattan.

Most patients with sexual disorders have received brief psychodynamically oriented sex therapy.* In the beginning we rarely used psychoactive drugs, but by 1980 we had added antipanic medication on a regular basis to the treatment regimen of patients with sexual dysfunctions who also had panic disorders.

During the past 10 years we have treated 51 patients with these dual syndromes with sex therapy in conjunction with antipanic medication. We were thus in a unique position to observe the effects of antipanic drugs on the various aspects of psychosexual therapy, and to compare the process of therapy before and after we began using these drugs.

Our experience leaves little doubt that the arguments between the psychopharmacologic and psychotherapeutic approaches are based on false premises. When viewed from a psychodynamic perspective, and also with the dynamics of the couple's relationship in mind, it becomes quite clear that both psychotherapy and medication have an important but entirely different function in the treatment of sexual anxiety states and that *both* are needed to help patients with drug-responsive sexual anxiety. Neither the most astutely devised behavioral program nor the most insightful, sensitive psychoanalysis can possibly normalize a brain's biologically abnormal alarm system. Yet medication alone can never take the place of skilled, caring and empathic psychotherapeutic intervention. Protecting a patient from panic chemically does not automatically cure long-standing avoidance of living and loving, nor can drugs by themselves resolve inner sexual conflicts or marital difficulties. However, under certain circumstances the effects of these agents enable previously resistant patients to respond to the sex therapy process.

When used for the appropriate indications, within an eclectic conceptual framework that acknowledges the biologic as well as psycho-

---

* Patients and couples who were not suitable for brief treatment received psychodynamically oriented long-term individual, marital or group therapy.

dynamic aspects of sexual psychopathology, the psychological and medical therapies often act with surprising synergy. Immense benefits can result from combined treatment.

Antipanic drugs are valuable adjuvants for the behavioral modification of the sexual symptoms that are associated with phobic-anxiety states. Our experience suggests that these agents could also potentiate the effectiveness of the dynamic therapies for fostering positive changes in the patient's personality and basic improvements in the relationships of some of these couples.

The old prejudices are irrational and do a disservice to patients and couples who could benefit from a combined approach. I believe that the integrated use of drugs and dynamic therapy is the treatment of the future for patients with drug-responsive emotional syndromes.

The antipanic drugs have given us a new weapon for our struggle against sexual inadequacy that enhances the therapeutic effectiveness of both medical and non-medical clinicians who work with patients and couples with sexual disorders. For these reasons, it is important for professionals who specialize in sexual health care, regardless of their particular discipline, to acquire a comprehensive understanding of the biological as well as the psychological aspects of sexual psychopathology, and to educate themselves about the indications, benefits, risks, and limitations of both medication and psychotherapy in order to provide optimal services for their patients.

CHAPTER 2

Clinical Features:
The Sexual Avoidance
Syndromes
and Panic Disorder

Sexual panic states are characterized by an intense and irrational fear of sex and a compelling desire to avoid sexual situations. These syndromes have variously been termed *the phobic avoidance of sex, sexual aversion,* and *sexual phobia.*

The American Psychiatric Association's committee to revise the category of psychosexual dysfunctions has suggested that *sexual aversion disorder* (302.79) be included in the revised edition (DSM-III-R) of DSM-III (1980) under the general category of disorders of sexual desire. This syndrome is defined as *a persistent or recurrent extreme discomfort with or avoidance of all, or almost all, genital sexual contact with a sexual partner.* The sexual aversion is a significant source of distress and may seriously restrict the individual's ability to function sexually and/or to experience normal sexual or romantic relationships.*

The following definition of sexual phobia, adapted from the diagnostic criteria for simple phobia (300.29) described in DSM-III (1980), page 229, is similar:

> The essential feature of a (sexual) phobia is the persistent, irrational fear of and compelling desire to avoid (sexual) experiences and or feelings. The fear is recognized by the individual as excessive and unreasonable in proportion to the actual dangerousness of the situation. The phobic avoidance (of sex) is a significant source of distress and may seriously restrict the individual's ability to func-

---

* From the proceedings of the American Psychiatric Association work group to revise DSM-III. New York, 1985.

10

tion (sexually) and/or to experience normal (sexual or romantic relationships).*

It is not clear to me whether sexual phobia and aversion are two discrete disorders which require different therapeutic management or whether aversion is simply a form of sexual panic with especially intense autonomic reactions. At this time, I tend to conceptualize sexual aversion and phobic avoidance of sex as two clinical variations of sexual panic states, and we currently treat patients in both categories in the same manner.

HYPOACTIVE SEXUAL DESIRE AND SEXUAL PANIC STATES

Schover and LoPiccolo (1982) have conceptualized sexual avoidance as lying on a continuum, with ISD or hypoactive sexual desire at the mild extreme, and sexual phobias and aversions at the most severe end point.

A case can be made for this essentially behavioral view. However, patients with sexual phobias and aversions may experience normal feelings of desire, and they can often fantasize and enjoy arousal and orgasm on masturbation. However, their partner's touch revolts them. On the other hand, those with hypoactive sexual desire (ISD) feel neutral about or even may like the physical contact that goes with sexual activity, but they are in a psychogenic state of "sexual anorexia" similar to that experienced by women after the surgical ablation of their androgen-producing ovarian and adrenal glands. These patients may continue to enjoy pleasuring their husbands and to find comfort in the physical intimacy sex affords, or more commonly quietly avoid sex.

Because of these dissimilarities in the subjective experience of patients with hypoactive sexual desire and those with sexual aversion, and also because the effects on a couple's relationship are very different, I have preferred to conceptualize hypoactive sexual desire (ISD) and the active aversion to sex as related but different syndromes.

During 1976 we saw 376 patients who complained about sexual avoidance on the part of one or both partners. We separated these into phobic avoiders, who experience panic or aversion in sexual situations, and those who are not uncomfortable when they engage in sexual activity, but who avoid this because of a lack of interest.

We found that 25 percent of patients with phobic avoidance also met

---

* The parentheses are the author's (HSK).

the criteria for panic disorder, while the incidence was only 3 percent in quiet avoiders (see Table 2). This difference is significant and lends support to the notion of a dichotomy.

Clinical Presentation

An element of phobic avoidance plays a role in and complicates all psychosexual dysfunctions, but it is the essential feature of true sexual phobias. For example, a premature ejaculator may appear to avoid sexual opportunities, but though he may overreact his performance fears have a basis in reality. When their sexual symptoms improve in treatment, dysfunctional patients with secondary sexual avoidance rapidly begin to develop a sense of sexual confidence and soon begin to look forward to sex. On the other hand, the phobic avoidance of patients with sexual panic disorders is not related to a real sexual disability, and the compelling urge of these patients to avoid sex does not diminish, and may even increase, although on an intellectual level they realize that they can now function adequately and their partner is satisfied.

Sexual phobia and aversion can exist in the absence of any functional difficulties or may be seen together with other genital phase dysfunctions. The coexistence of these secondary problems may obscure the diagnosis of sexual aversion, especially when the couple presents with other complaints. However, sexual panic states require a specific treatment approach and it is essential to identify these syndromes precisely in order to treat them successfully.

Total and situational phobias

Some patients are totally phobic of sex and experience panics or revulsion in response to any and all erotic sensations, feelings, thoughts,

TABLE 2

Prevalence of Hypoactive Sexual Desire (ISD) in Patients
with Sexual Avoidance*

	ISD		*Without ISD*	
Phobic avoiders (N = 106)	9	8%	97	92%
Quiet avoiders (N = 267)	68	26%	199	74%
All patients who avoid sex (N = 373)	77	21%	296	79%

* These patients were evaluated in our programs between 1976 and 1986.
Sig. <.001

and opportunities. Even subtle sexual references or situations such as romantic films with erotic nuances might disturb severely sexaphobic individuals.

In other cases, the patient's phobic response is limited to a specific aspect of sex. The following sexual phobias are commonly seen in clinical practice:

The genitalia of the opposite sex
The patient's own genitalia
Being penetrated
Penetrating
Heterosexual activity
Homosexual activity
Sexual fantasies
Sexual secretions and odors (semen, vaginal fluid)
Sexual failure (performance panic)
Sexual arousal (fear of loss of control)
Orgasm (fear of loss of control)
Breast touching
Kissing
Partner rejection or belittlement
Undressing (being seen nude)
Seeing the partner undressed (nude)
Oral sex (giving or receiving)
Anal sex (penetration or being penetrated)
Pleasure
Erotic pleasure
Commitment to one partner
Intimacy and closeness
Falling in love and being loved

Patients with circumscribed sexual phobias may enjoy sex and function normally as long as they can manage to avoid their particular phobia. For example, women with penetration phobias panic only when they attempt intercourse. Providing that they are certain that these will not lead to vaginal penetration, they may fully enjoy all other sexual activities and are often sensitive and responsive lovers. Such patients may have experienced normal responses during the preintercourse phases of their sexual development, enjoying kissing, body caressing and genital stimulation, sometimes to orgasm. The problem may surface for the first time, and often to the patient's own surprise, during the honeymoon.

Intensity of the phobic response

Patients with sexual phobia and aversion disorders will avoid sex as far as this is possible, but sometimes they get "trapped" into having sex by a partner's pressure, by the fear of losing the partner, or by their love for him. Once they are actually in the sexual situation, there is considerable diversity in the intensity of the fear or aversion that sexaphobics experience.

Patients with mild phobias are able to calm themselves and once they push themselves past the barrier of their anticipatory anxiety and avoidance, are even able to enjoy sex, sometimes to the point of orgasm. Paradoxically, such positive experiences do nothing to diminish the sexual phobic avoidance and these patients are often puzzled by their continuing and compelling urge to avoid sex despite the enjoyment and gratification they experience once they allow themselves to get involved.

Those with more severe phobic responses become so anxious that they cannot function nor feel erotic sensations. However, if they make the effort to do so, such individuals can often make themselves fairly comfortable by detaching themselves or by averting their attention from the erotic aspects of the experience. Some, while feeling little pleasure themselves, can go so far as to focus on and enjoy the intimate, physical contact with their partners, and are gratified by the pleasure they give them. Others feel used and angry when they continue to experience nothing, while their partners always have a good time.

Still other patients become so panicked and uncomfortable, experiencing such intensely aversive feelings during the sexual act, that they cannot detach themselves. They merely endure the experience as best they can, comforting themselves with the thought that it can't last indefinitely and that no real harm will come to them. One patient told me it was very much like being in the dentist's chair, knowing that if she could just hold on it would be over soon.

Patients with severe sexual phobias may experience true panic attacks complete with the physical symptoms of autonomic discharge if they find themselves in a sexual situation. Feelings of terror, impending doom, palpitations, difficulty in breathing, faintness, feelings of depersonalization, amnesia, and actual loss of consciousness have been reported, while all feel an urgent wish to escape.

The experience of patients with aversion disorders is possibly even more distressing. In addition to a complete absence of any erotic pleasure, these patients experience intense disgust and revulsion when they are touched. Some report tremulousness and nausea, and actual vomiting is not uncommon. Patients with severe aversion cannot tolerate the slightest physical contact with the partner, even in a totally nonerotic context. Some report great psychic pain: "I felt as though I had been violated, raped," *after* a sexual experience. These "afterpains" can last from a few hours to several days.

Although some patients with simple sexual phobias who have a normal capacity for panic experience very intense panic and aversive feelings, the more severe and prolonged reactions that were described above are more commonly seen in patients with concomitant panic disorders.

Anticipatory anxiety and avoidance patterns

The distinction between the phobic reaction itself and anticipatory anxiety is very important in understanding and treating phobic patients. All phobic patients, those who have an underlying phobic anxiety syndrome and those with simple phobias, characteristically develop anticipatory anxiety and learn to avoid their phobic object. For instance, patients with claustrophobia will go to great lengths to avoid closed places. For the same reasons, sexaphobic individuals try to avoid sex whenever possible. These avoidance patterns are a major obstacle to the treatment of sexual phobias.

Sexaphobic patients with sexual phobias become very nervous when they are about to face situations where it will be difficult for them to avoid sex. They get so flooded with anxious apprehension that they feel none of the pleasurable anticipation most people experience before a date or party, or a romantic evening at home, and they think only of escape. Sometimes sexual anticipatory anxiety takes on the dimensions of an obsession and the individual's preoccupation with his sexual anxiety may interfere with his work and his social life.

In describing her experience, which is quite typical, a married woman with a phobic avoidance of sex and panic disorder told me: "When we haven't had sex for a week or so, I start getting anxious and worried because I know he will want it soon. Coming home from work on the bus, I will start to obsess: 'What if he wants sex tonight? God, he will really get mad if I refuse again. I'll try to distract him. Maybe I should invite the Smiths for supper. He'll get all involved with them and forget about sex. Maybe I'll get him a steak and make him his favorite dessert.' By the time I get home I'm a wreck. Sometimes I take a drink, sometimes I binge eat and get myself sick. Sometimes, when it is inevitable I knock myself out with pot, then it's a little easier. I feel like a very selfish person. He is really very good to me. He's only asking for what he's entitled to."

Patients with sexual phobias and aversions develop ingenious and varied avoidance strategies. Ordinarily they do not refuse to have sex in a straightforward manner, but conceal their avoidance by making themselves unavailable physically and emotionally for sex and intimacy. They hide out in the office and when they are home, they remove themselves with compulsive tasks, lengthy telephone calls, or obsessive watching of television, which is possibly the most widely used method of sexual avoidance of our modern society. They use the children, leaving the bedroom door open at all times "in case the kids need us." They may arrange a frantic round of social and family activities which never allows the couple to be alone together. Some have learned to turn off their partners by subtly insuring that sex will be tedious or pressured. They make themselves unattractive by becoming fat or by neglecting their appearance and hygiene. At home they will wear curlers, face cream, and old bathrobes, and will shave and shower or brush their teeth only when they go out. Still others cloud their consciousness with alcohol and other substances. Patients may actually become ill and develop somatic symptoms, which help them escape the dreaded sexual ordeal. The famous quote, "Not tonight dear, I have a headache," is no joke in these marriages.

Patients who are not married or in relationships must develop tactics to avoid potential sexual partners as well as sex and this is potentially much more damaging. Some women date but refuse to engage in sex on religious or moral grounds, and confine their relationships to people with similar values who will respect their wish to remain virgins. Others will behave in subtle nonsexual ways that discourage romantic advances. They become "pals" to members of the opposite sex, or they become obsessively attracted to totally unavailable individuals. They may sabotage their own sexual attractiveness by acting, dressing, and conducting themselves in a sexually unappealing manner. Some avoid sex by becoming obese and some by becoming obsessed with their work or avocation. The most extreme and tragic expressions of the phobic avoidance of sex are seen in individuals who remain virgins and single all their lives.

Insight

Some patients have insight into the fact that fears of sex are irrational and beyond their control. These fortunate individuals are in a position to work on their sexual fears directly and to defuse their partners' distress by discussing their problem openly.

But more often phobic patients have no insight into their irrational fears and avoidances and attempt to explain their situations to themselves with palatable rationalizations. But this seldom works. Individuals who deny their problems cannot improve their situation. In such cases the first issue in treatment is to confront patients with their irrational sexual avoidance.

Primary and secondary phobia and aversion

The patients' sexual history will reveal whether their problem is primary or secondary. Patients with the primary sexual panic states have always found sex frightening or repulsive, while those with the secondary variety acquire the phobic response after enjoying a period of normal sexual functioning.

Crenshaw draws a sharp distinction between primary and secondary sexual aversion (Crenshaw, 1985). She reports that in her patient population primary aversion was associated with more serious psychopathology, was more prevalent in men, and was more difficult to treat than secondary aversion. In her experience, the secondary form of this disorder occurs more frequently in women, is always associated with conflicts about love or commitment, and has a far more favorable prognosis.

With a few exceptions, our experience agrees with Crenshaw's. However, one of our patients developed a global loss of sexual desire and an aversion to sex with all partners after he was traumatized by a totally unexpected rejection by his wife. In another case, a stunning business triumph precipitated sexual avoidance in a man with an underlying fear of success. Also, we have seen several cases of primary sexual avoidance in patients without serious psychopathology. For example, Rosa, who was described in the first clinical vignette (see p. 4), was a well-functioning woman in an excellent marriage.

This patient had been devoid of sexual feelings for as long as she could remember. Popular with her peers prior to puberty, she began to feel "different" from her friends and was perplexed when they became interested in sex. She recalls being surprised that her little girlfriends enjoyed kissing and petting games with boys, since she felt "nothing" during these activities. Puzzled, she often asked her friends, "What are you *supposed* to feel? *Why* do you enjoy it?" Initially, Rosa felt merely "strange" about kissing and touching, but she became progressively more anxious and aversive. By the time she began to date Richard in college, she had developed a severe sexual panic and her avoidance of sex almost caused a rupture of the relationship.

Sexual aversion typically begins insidiously. After the couple have enjoyed a period of good sex, the symptomatic partner gradually finds herself progressively avoiding sex. Denial and rationalization are common in the early stages. In the usual clinical course, the partner will eventually begin to object and to pressure the symptomatic patient for sex. This intensifies the patient's panic and revulsion to a point where sex may become intolerable for her. If she tries to force herself to make love to her partner, despite her negative feelings, the condition is likely to become worse. Under these circumstances, the patient may develop secondary functional difficulties.

Usually, patients with secondary forms of this syndrome avoid sex only with the partner with whom they have a committed relationship. However, some patients are repelled by any potentially suitable partner, as is illustrated in the following case vignette.

Case Vignette #2: Greta G.

This beautiful, 36-year-old woman had been married for 13 years to a scion of one of Texas's richest oil families. They had one child, to whom they were both devoted. The couple complained about Greta's depression and her strong aversion to sex.

Her history revealed a classic panic disorder, complete with spontaneous panics, multiple phobias, and a family history of "nervousness." Her symptoms had not improved after three years of psychoanalytically oriented psychotherapy.

Mrs. G.'s aversion was so severe that she could not bear her husband's slightest touch. She even felt repelled when he took her hand to help her into the automobile, and she had had a 10-foot-wide bed especially constructed to avoid any accidental contact between them during the night. She used the pretext of interior design for this project.

Despite the intensity of their sexual problem, the couple's marriage was basically good. She felt affection for and appreciated her husband, who was charming and generous, although she resented his arrogant attitudes toward women and servants. But she never criticized him and except for avoiding sex with him, she was solicitous and affectionate to him in every other way. She felt guilty about depriving her husband sexually and she had become increasingly depressed and anorexic, having lost 25 lbs. during the prior year.

George was deeply attracted to his wife and while being much too much of a Southern gentleman to pressure her for sex, was extremely frustrated and also truly worried about her wellbeing.

Greta had had a normal sexual development, and she had enjoyed two brief and pleasurable premarital affairs. She had met her husband at a dance and she recalled that when he took her hand to lead her to the dance floor, she felt an instant revulsion such as she had never felt before. But she also knew at that moment that he was attracted to her and that she would marry him.

Greta had a classic panic disorder with spontaneous panic attacks, multiple phobias, and separation anxiety related to her children and her mother.

An Austrian refugee, she was raised by her ambitious, competitive widowed mother. Her daughter's marrying into American "royalty" fulfilled her mother's wildest narcissistic fantasies, and the patient felt compelled to accede.

During her marriage, Greta had once been intensely attracted to another man. She had one lunch date with him and panicked, frightened by her passionate feelings. She worried about a potential scandal should she give in to the sexual temptation, and she ended the luncheon abruptly. Since that time her avoidance of sex had intensified and widened so that she no longer masturbated, nor did she permit herself erotic fantasies. She had even become uncomfortable at social gatherings where she might encounter attractive men.

After her few tentative attempts to communicate her sexual needs to her husband had fallen on deaf ears, she gave up trying to improve their sexual relationship. From then on she made a concentrated effort to hide her revulsion from her husband. She bore this silently for 11 years in order to spare him pain and protect her child from the stress of family discord. However, during the past year her aversive feelings had grown so intense, that she could no longer pretend.

The Impact of Sexual Avoidance

A phobia of snakes or elevators is not likely to disrupt a person's life too much, but sex is a core experience of human existence and its avoidance can be profoundly destructive.

The avoidance of sexual gratification is distressing enough. But sex is much more than a physical release. Love, companionship, marriage, children, and family may all have to be sacrificed when the fear of sex governs a person's life. Being single and virginal in a highly sexual and couples-oriented world poses serious problems for an individual, and it is exceedingly painful to be alone when everyone else around seems to be paired and enjoying sex.

The ultimate price that a sexual phobia will exact will depend on the compromise that the individual makes between his wish to gratify his sexual needs and to lead a normal family life on the one hand and his compelling urge to avoid sex in order to protect himself from panic on the other.

Some patients are able to form relationships despite their aversion to sex and marriage, and manage to marry, have families, and lead normal lives in all respects except sex. Such individuals learn to circumvent their sexual avoidance by finding supportive partners, often partners who are attracted to them because of their own problems, as is illustrated in the following case vignette.

Case Vignette #3: Mr. & Mrs. B.

The Bs, an affluent couple in their fifties, complain that Mrs. B. has never liked sex.

Mrs. B. states that she has always found sex exceedingly unpleasant and she has limited her husband to having sexual intercourse once a month. She barely endures this monthly "ordeal" and during the act consoles herself with the thought that it will not last very long and that she will now be "safe" for awhile. Mr. B., who is very attracted to his wife, has been chronically frustrated by her avoidance and has pressured her unceasingly for sex since they were married 27 years ago.

Mrs. B. has never been aroused or had an orgasm, with or without a partner. She has never masturbated and does not have the slightest desire to do so. She experiences a sense of disbelief when she hears that other people enjoy sex.

Mrs. B. has no illness or hormonal imbalances and she is taking no drugs with sexual side effects which could account for her hypoactive desire and aversion to sex on a physical basis.

Apart from her primary sexual aversion, Mrs. B. is a happy woman who functions well and enjoys her family, friends, and charitable activities. Mr. B. is also free of significant psychopathology. He is a successful retailer with a high energy level and a cheerful disposition. Neither spouse has panic disorder.

Except for the sexual problem, the marriage is excellent. Mrs.

B. admires and loves her husband, but expresses anger about his sexual demands.

Mr. B. is clearly deeply in love with his wife, but he is in a chronic rage because of her sexual avoidance.

Mrs. B. has found a partner who tolerates her sexual problem because this complements his own unconscious neurotic needs.

Mr. B. has always had a stormy relationship with his mother, whom he describes as insensitive, demanding, controlling, and selfish. He has always sought to win her approval by acceding to her every wish and by achieving considerable success and affluence. But he has never succeeded. She remains critical of him to this day, which still infuriates him.

His wife's sexual avoidance tapped into Mr. B's unresolved conflict with his mother. Her eventual "surrender" to his sexual demands after weeks of struggle represented a "sexual victory" over his mother. On another level, sex with his wife symbolizes maternal approval and love which he had always longed for, but which had always eluded him. His monthly sexual "conquest" was his "reward" for being a "good boy" and this gratified him deeply on an unconscious level, compensating for the frustration of living with a sexually aversive partner.

Many patients with primary sexual phobias and aversions have an uncanny ability to find partners whose unconscious needs are satisfied by their sexual avoidance and with whom they can work out a good fit. But without such neurotic gains for the partner, these relationships do not work. A healthy person cannot develop a gratifying marriage with someone who consistently and chronically frustrates him sexually despite his best efforts. He either leaves or, if he is locked into the relationship by his separation anxieties, develops unhappy, ambivalent compromises.

The next case vignette demonstrates the more serious clinical course of sexually aversive patients who remain virgins and do not marry.

Case Vignette #4: Ms. C.

Ms. C., a 52-year-old single woman from a working class, orthodox Jewish background, lived with her physically disabled sister who was also single. The patient had a primary sexual aversion disorder. She did not remember spontaneous panic attacks, but her history has other stigmata of an atypical panic disorder. She had multiple phobias in addition to her sexual phobia (heights, driving over bridges, insects), a history of school avoidance, and ill-defined, but severe psychopathology in two close family members.

The patient was a virgin who had never had a romantic relationship; in fact, she had never allowed a man to kiss her. In her early 20s she had dated a few times, but each time a man had made the slightest sexual advance she experienced panic and revulsion, feeling that she could not breathe and that she would choke and faint. Each experience had intensified her aversion to and avoidance of sex. Ms. C. has not dated in 25 years and to this day feels uncomfortable in and avoids social situations where she might meet an eligible man. Her avoidance is specific to sex with a partner; she enjoys masturbating to orgasm while she fantasizes about making love to a man. However, she feels empty and depressed after these masturbatory experiences that underscore the loneliness of her life.

Ms. C. heads a successful employment agency and her earnings are sufficient to support herself and her sister in comfort. She enjoys close friendships with several women and is very attached to her nieces and nephews. A highly intelligent and sensitive woman, Ms. C. has a deep interest in the theatre and the arts. Despite these accomplishments and gratifications, she is chronically depressed and bitter, taking little pleasure in her success at work and her popularity with family and friends. In the orthodox Jewish community, marriage is considered the only viable and honorable option for a woman. Ms. C. has internalized these cultural values, judges herself to be a failure, and feels that her life has been a waste. She is distracted from her pervasive feelings of shame, despair, and anger only when she immerses herself in her work and her cultural and family activities.

Why do some persons with sexual panic disorders manage to find partners who tolerate their sexual avoidance and to make a good life for themselves, while others lead empty, lonely, and virginal existences? The answer to this important question is, of course, complex, but in the final analysis will be determined by the relative intensities of the patient's sexual aversion and his or her motivation to marry.

Sex is horrendously difficult and painful for patients with the more severe sexual aversions, and a person has to be highly motivated to risk facing the constant exposure to sex that is entailed in marriage. Marriage for the sexaphobic is analogous to a career that entails the daily cleaning of reptile cages for a person who is phobic of snakes.

He will only accept such a job if this is absolutely the only available means of survival. Similarly, if a sexually phobic person sees no other option in life, she might feel compelled to take a husband. However, if there are viable alternatives, she is likely to avoid marriage.

When a person's sexual aversion is associated with an underlying ambivalence or rage towards members of the opposite gender, the probability that the sexaphobic individual will marry is also greatly diminished. Mrs. B., the patient previously described, was raised in a stable, upper middleclass family and was pampered by her father. She basically liked men, trusted her husband, and enjoyed sharing her life with him.

By contrast, Ms. C. felt a deep ambivalence towards men, which militated against marrying. This patient's negative view of men had its root in her unresolved hatred of her father, who was described as "psychotic." The patient's father never held a steady job, and moved in and out of mental hospitals until his death when the patient was 14. When he came home, he embarrassed the family by sitting all day long in his underwear in the kitchen, which was the only public room. He usually stayed just long enough at each visit to impregnate the patient's mother and intimidate the children with his violent temper.

The patient's mother was a simple, loving woman, who, despite her lack of education, struggled valiantly to support the family materially and emotionally. The patient was very close to her mother and identified with her. Not surprisingly, this pathological family environment created a negative image of men and an ambivalence towards marriage for the two little girls. Neither the patient nor her sister married, while all three brothers have families.

Many patients who avoid marriage rather than face their sexual anxieties, like Ms. C., suffer destructive personality changes and loss of self-esteem. They carry deep within themselves a rage and pain and the sense that their lives have been wasted. But it should be emphasized that virginity and bachelorhood are not necessarily destructive. Some segments of our society place high values on endeavors apart from family life, giving the sexually aversive individual the option to choose a single lifestyle without the loss of prestige or self-esteem. As long as these individuals can sublimate their sexuality without resentment, they can make excellent adaptations and lead gratifying and productive lives—for example, by devoting themselves to their religion or good works or political ideals, or by making a deep commitment to art or science.

But individuals who do not have such resources or choices may not be able to handle the dilemma posed by their sexual fears. The next case vignette illustrates the agony experienced by a man with primary sexual avoidance who was unable to overcome his fear of sex, yet found virginity and sexual failure unacceptable.

Case Vignette #5: Mr. D.

Here is a 29-year-old Protestant, construction worker seen in the emergency room after a suicide attempt. His history indicated an untreated panic disorder. The patient had never had sexual intercourse. He was obsessed with this problem and despaired of ever having a normal life. Over the last three years his alcohol consumption had been progressively increasing to a point where he had developed a serious drinking problem.

Mr. D. has suffered from a severe phobic avoidance of sex since adolescence. His anticipatory anxiety and avoidance extend to all social contacts with women. He has never dated; in fact, in high school he would flee across the street when attractive girls from his class approached. He is so uncomfortable in the presence of young women that he immediately leaves any social situations, such as family weddings or holidays, if he finds that an eligible woman is present. After such "escapes," he is likely to get drunk.

Mr. D.'s sex drive is high and his avoidance is specific to sex with a partner. He masturbates three or four times a week to pictures of nude women from erotic magazines. He has been obsessed with his virginity and envies men with normal sex lives. He has become preoccupied with these thoughts to the extent that his job has suffered. Once, nine years ago, he sought sex with a prostitute. On that occasion he panicked and could not function. This experience precipitated his obsession about his sexual inadequacy and intensified his phobic avoidance of sex. He has never made another attempt to have a sexual experience.

SEXUAL AVERSION AND PANIC DISORDERS

Not all persons with panic disorder develop sexual difficulties, but those who do are likely to have more severe and complicated problems. Sexual disorders that are associated with panic states are more difficult to treat, and treatment may fail unless antipanic medication is prescribed and sexual therapy is modified to accommodate the special needs of these patients.

For these reasons, it is extremely important to determine during the initial evaluation whether the patient who presents with sexual phobia or aversion also has an associated drug-responsive anxiety disorder.

There is as yet no practical laboratory test that will detect panic disorder. The diagnosis, as well as the decision about using medication, must be made on clinical grounds alone.*

Diagnostic Criteria

DSM-III (American Psychiatric Association, 1980) describes the following criteria for panic disorder (p. 230):

Panic disorder (300.01): The essential features are recurrent panic (anxiety) attacks that occur at times unpredictably though certain situations, e.g. driving the car (or sex),** may become associated with panic attacks. The same clinical picture occurring during marked physical exertion*** or a life-threatening situation is not termed a panic attack.

The panic attacks are manifested by the sudden onset of intense apprehension, fear, or terror, often associated with feelings of impending doom. The most common symptoms experienced during an attack are: dyspnea; palpitations; chest pain or discomfort; choking or smothering sensations; dizziness; vertigo or unsteady feelings; feelings of unreality (depersonalization or derealization); paresthesias; hot and cold flashes; sweating; faintness; trembling or shaking; the fear of dying, going crazy or doing something uncontrolled during the attack. The attack usually lasts minutes, more rarely, hours.

A common complication of this disorder is the development of an anticipatory fear of helplessness or loss of control during a panic attack, so that the individual becomes reluctant to be alone or in public places away from home.

Associated Features. The individual often develops varying degrees of nervousness and apprehension between attacks. The ner-

---

* Intravenous infusions of sodium lactate precipitate panic attacks in patients with panic disorder but not in normals (Gorman et al., 1981b). When protected by TCA's, patients with panic disorder do not show this response. A similar sensitivity to lactate is shown by patients who do not have the classical signs of panic disorder but who experience symptoms of panic when they exercise and presumably build up lactate in their bloodstream. The role of sodium lactate in panic disorder is not yet understood and this fascinating experimental procedure is still too cumbersome for clinical use.

** DSM-III specifically excludes sexual phobias from the category of phobic disorder. The inclusion of sexual phobias is the author's (HSK).

*** It may be speculated that symptoms of panic during physical exertion could be provoked by a buildup of sodium lactate (Pitts & McClune, 1967) and may represent an atypical manifestation of panic disorder.

vousness and apprehension are characterized by the usual manifestations of apprehensive expectation, vigilance and scanning,
motor tension, and autonomic hyperactivity.

Age of Onset. The disorder often begins in late adolescence or
early adult life, but may occur initially in mid-adult life.

Course. This disorder may be limited to a single brief period
lasting several weeks or months, reoccur several times, or become
chronic. . . .

Complications. The complication of agoraphobia with panic attacks is common. Other complications include abuse of alcohol
and antianxiety medications, as well as depressive disorders, (eating
disorders, obsessive-compulsive personality disorders, the avoidance
of romantic relationships and marriage).*

Predisposing Factors: Separation Anxiety Disorder in childhood
and sudden object loss apparently predisposes to the development
of this disorder . . .

Sex Ratio: This condition is diagnosed much more commonly
in women.

Differential Diagnosis: Physical disorders such as hypoglycemia,
pheochromocytoma, hypothyroidism, (certain CNS disorders) all
of which can cause similar symptoms, must be ruled out.**

In withdrawal from such substances as barbiturates and in some
substance intoxications, such as those due to caffeine or amphetamines,
there may be panic attacks. These may occur, also, in schizophrenia,
major depression, or socialization disorder. Generalized anxiety disorder
and also simple or social phobia may be confused with panic disorder
because the person may develop panic attacks if he is exposed to the
phobic stimulus.

DSM-III summarizes the clinical criteria for panic disorder as follows:

A. At least three panic attacks within a three-week period in
circumstances other than during marked physical exertion or in

---

* The parenthesized inclusions are the author's.

** Patients who complain about symptoms of panic must receive a medical examination
to rule out the serious medical disorders mentioned above. The clinician should be
particularly alert to the presence of mitral valve prolapse. A high proportion (up to 20%)
of patients with mitral prolapse have been found to have panic disorder (Gorman, et al.,
1981a). An echocardiogram will establish this diagnosis. Although many patients with
mitral valve prolapse never develop any serious problems, they should be under the care
of a cardiologist in order to prevent unnecessary complications. It is especially important
to protect patients with mitral valve prolapse against endocarditis by prescribing pro-
phylactic antibiotics prior to minor surgical procedures, such as professional tooth cleaning.
Patients with mitral prolapse and panic disorder respond favorably to tricyclic medication,
but special complications may arise because these drugs sometimes cause cardiotoxicity
at higher doses.

a life-threatening situation. The attacks are not precipitated only by exposure to circumscribed phobic stimulus.

B. Panic attacks are manifested by discrete periods of apprehension or fear and at least four of the following symptoms appear during each attack:

1. Dyspnea
2. Palpitations
3. Chest pain or discomfort
4. Choking or smothering sensations
5. Dizziness, vertigo or unsteady feelings
6. Feelings of unreality
7. Paresthesias (tingling in hands or feet)
8. Hot or cold flashes
9. Sweating
10. Faintness
11. Trembling or shaking
12. Fear of dying, going crazy, or doing something uncontrolled during the attack (pp. 231-232)

Atypical and Subclinical Forms of Panic Disorder

According to DSM-III, the diagnosis of panic disorder is warranted only if the patient has experienced spontaneous panic attacks. However, a number of our patients with sexual aversion disorders who did not recall panic attacks but had other features of panic disorder (see Table 3) appeared to become too anxious to benefit from sex therapy much like those who meet the criteria for classic panic disorder. In some of these cases we attribute the successful treatment outcome to their good responses to medication.

On the assumption that Klein's theory is correct, one could think of a number of reasons why some sexually phobic anxious patients who

TABLE 3

Prevalence of Atypical Panic Disorder in Patients with Sexual Avoidance*

	Atypical Panic		Classical Panic		Without Panic	
Phobic avoiders (N = 106)	41	38%	26	25%	39	37%
Quiet avoiders (N = 267)	14	5%	9	3%	244	92%
All patients who avoid sex (N = 373)	55	15%	35	9%	283	76%

* These patients were evaluated in our programs between 1976 and 1986.
Sig. <.001

did not report classical spontaneous panic attacks could have responded to medication.

Perhaps some simply forgot or repressed their panic attacks. Some patients I have seen have learned to abort their panics before they reach conscious awareness.

Other patients experience their panic attacks in atypical ways and seem to have panic equivalents that do not conform to the DSM-III criteria exactly (American Psychiatric Association, 1980, p. 230).

It is also possible that the spontaneous discharges of the alarm system occur in severe panic disorders only, while individuals with mild or subclinical forms or "formes frustes" do not experience spontaneous discharges, although they have excessive residual separation anxiety and other features of the syndrome. Possibly, individuals whose panic attacks occur only on physical effort, presumably when the Ph of their blood is altered and/or their serum *lactic acid* levels increase, could represent such a mild subclinical variety of panic disorder.

These admittedly uncontrolled clinical observations raise the possibility that the coincidence of panic disorder with the more severe forms of sexual aversion is extremely high. In our population 25 percent of phobic avoiders met the DSM-III criteria for panic disorder (see Table 1). If patients with atypical signs of panic disorder are included, this rises to 63 percent (see Table 3). If the notion of an atypical drug-responsive anxiety disorder were to prove valid, it would suggest that patients' reports of spontaneous panic attacks are too unreliable to serve as the sole basis for decisions about using or not using medication and that the diagnostic criteria specified in DSM-III might have to be reconsidered to avoid excluding some drug-responsive patients who ought to be medicated.

Based on this theory, and considering that the risk of using these drugs is so low while they can be so beneficial, it is my practice to consider medication for patients with sexual symptoms who are not showing satisfactory progress in therapy, even though they do not report spontaneous panic attacks, if they meet the following criteria: (1) They have or have had one or more other phobias in addition to their sexual phobia or aversion, and (2) one or more of the following:

(a) atypical panic equivalents;
(b) more than one addiction to tranquilizers, stimulants, or alcohol, or an eating disorder;
(c) a history of excessive separation anxiety during childhood, and/ or evidence of significant separation problems in adult love relationships;

(d) features that suggest possible genetic predisposition to panic disorder: panic disorder in biologically related family members, mitral valve prolapse.

A history of unsuccessful psychodynamic, behavioral or marital therapy for anxiety, phobias and separation problems, and/or poor response to minor and/or major tranquilizers are also "soft signs" of drug-responsive anxiety states.

For example, we medicated a 48-year-old man with a phobic avoidance of sex with his wife. He denied spontaneous panic attacks. However, he reported experiences that could have been manifestations of atypical panic equivalents. He would become restless and uncomfortable, and experience, "strange and painful sensations" in his testicles and lower abdomen. At these times, he found relief by binge eating and/or compulsively and repeatedly masturbating to a sado-masochistic fantasy. He also had a flying phobia and a history of separation problems as a child. The patient's sexual complaint had not improved with psychotherapy (2 years) or with psychoanalysis (8 years), nor was a course of conjoint sexual therapy helpful. Valium had provided only fleeting relief. He responded to a combination of Tofranil 250 mgm. and dynamically oriented sexual psychotherapy with a marked improvement in his sexual symptom.

DESTRUCTIVE AVOIDANCE PATTERNS AND CONSTRUCTIVE ADAPTATIONS

The key to the psychopathology of panic disorder lies not so much in the specific phobic symptom, as in the extent and nature of the avoidance patterns that the patient develops in the attempt to cope with his panics. Panic attacks are generally transitory and seldom disabling, but the impact of this disorder can be profoundly destructive if the patient has acquired the habit of avoiding important areas of life.

There is considerable diversity in how well individuals with panic disorders handle their handicap. Some compensate so effectively that apart from an occasional panic attack and some trivial circumscribed phobias, they lead essentially normal lives. Others are virtually crippled by their compelling need to avoid their anxieties at the cost of their long-range goals.

Several studies of patients with panic disorder indicate that many of these individuals have been vulnerable to excessive separation anxiety since early childhood (Weissman et al., 1984; Gittelman-Klein & Klein,

1980). Apparently this can occur in the absence of a specific trauma, losses or family pathology, and evidence that suggests a possible genetic predisposition is accumulating.

The develomental histories of our patients with panic disorders and sexual aversions support the notion that these youngsters have a constitutional vulnerability, but suggest that parental attitudes can exert a great deal of influence on the clinical course and ultimate outcome of this predisposition.

Family attitudes towards these anxious youngsters seem to polarize around one of three clusters that can be described as *rejecting, overprotecting,* or *constructively realistic.* Individuals with a low panic threshold who compensate well and who show little psychological or sexual damage often had parents with *constructively realistic* attitudes towards their excessive anxieties and separation problems. Those who do poorly as adults may have been either *rejected* or *overprotected* by their parents during the critical years of their early development on account of their emotional vulnerability.

Parental Rejection

Rejecting parents deny that there is anything wrong with their anxious children. They judge these vulnerable youngsters by the same standards that would apply to a child with a normal capacity for anxiety. Since they deny that the child's anxiety is beyond his control, they are angry with him for being anxious and are intolerant of his clinging behavior. They are disappointed with the child's difficulties with separations, regarding this as deliberately spoiled, willful, or naughty behavior. Making no allowance for his vulnerabilities, they enter into power struggles with him when he cries in terror at night, wants a light left on, persists trying to climb into bed with mother, or sobs bitterly when she leaves him with the babysitter. They seem to have no empathy for his experience and little sympathy for his pain, and they do not try to comfort him because they feel that this will spoil him further. They transmit the message that he is bad and cowardly and that he had better shape up.

The phobically anxious child reared in a family which finds his constitutional make-up objectionable may internalize these attitudes and grow up with a burden of self-hatred, shame, and guilt. These individuals never learned to make themselves comfortable and, in fact, may feel as their parents did that they don't deserve relief from their stresses. They stoically attempt to endure their anxieties and the limitations these have placed on their lives and do not ask for help easily.

Since they feel they are basically despicable, they are apprehensive about risking intimacy and openness and are likely to have poor interpersonal and romantic relationships or none at all.

For these reasons, "rejected" individuals may find it difficult to enlist a partner's cooperation, which presents problems in sex therapy. Since these individuals reject themselves as their parents once did and feel they deserve punishment, they do not generally resist the desensitization assignments, almost welcoming the discomforts this entails. However, their guilt about pleasure and their feelings that they are not entitled to comfort, happiness, and love tend to mobilize resistances as they begin to improve and experience sexual pleasure. The therapist's unwavering permission to have pleasure and to take care of themselves and her unambivalent message that sex is okay and their having pleasure gives her pleasure are very important therapeutic ingredients in resolving the pleasure conflicts of these emotionally-abused individuals.

It may be speculated that some of these rejecting parents have had difficulty in accepting their own separation anxieties and vulnerabilities and this blinds them to their children's problem. Also, since panic disorder tends to be familiar, many parents of anxious children have had to cope with their own panicky mothers and anxious fathers and siblings as they were growing up, and the notion that their youngster may have similar emotional difficulties can be very threatening. In addition, cultural attitudes that call on males especially to be courageous, macho and independent come into play. Whiners and complainers do not rate highly in a free enterprise society, but the rejecting parent's ill advised attempts to impart strength to his vulnerable child only debilitate him more.

Overprotection

Overprotective parents also deny their youngster's emotional handicap. These parents err in the opposite direction, but impart attitudes, messages, and behavior patterns that are just as detrimental to their child. Parents who end up overpowering their child tend to be highly empathic and overreact to their youngster's separation anxiety, denying that this is excessive. They will invent an endless array of rationalizations to account for the child's anxiety, often blaming themselves or their spouse. They make every effort to buffer their anxious child against the real world; protecting him from anxiety takes on a high priority in these families. Such overprotective parents will pay excessive attention to the child and try to include him, often inappropriately, in social activities in order to spare him the anxiety of being left at home alone. Overprotective mothers have difficulty frustrating their children and setting proper limits because frustration seems especially painful for them. For example, one mother for no other motive allowed her frightened child to sleep in bed with her for years, at the risk of disrupting her relationship with her husband.

Such empathy and sensitivity are, of course, wonderful in some respects. However, the child will pay a very high price if he gets the unrealistic message that he is entitled to perfect comfort and attention, and does not learn to deal with limits. The parental overidentification and overinvolvement with the child denies him the opportunity to learn to tolerate his anxiety and to face his fears, which is crucial in his learning to cope constructively with his panic disorder. He does not learn to take responsibility for making himself comfortable, but expects others to do this for him. He learns that it's "okay" to avoid anything that makes him nervous, acquires detrimental avoidance behaviors, may end up avoiding far too much in life, including sex, love, and success, and is likely to turn to addicting substances rather than face life.

In treatment, overprotected phobic patients tend to resist their sexual assignments when these make them anxious. However, it is very important that these individuals learn to face their fears if they are to obtain their goals. The therapist's acceptance of their abnormal sensitivities, along with her encouragement to tolerate a certain amount of anxiety, is essential in the treatment process: "I know that taking a shower with him made you nervous, but you did it anyway and I'm proud of you," transmits a corrective, realistic message which may benefit the patient far beyond facilitating a particular sexual assignment.

The overprotective parents' need to deny their child's handicap arises out of their wishful but erroneous assumption that he will "grow out of it" if given enough love and nurturing. But eventually even the most patient and sacrificial parents will become resentful when, despite all their efforts, their child does not develop a sense of independence. There is a point when the relationship between the overprotected and dependent phobic child and his parents reaches a crisis. These children become enraged and blame their parents when they find that they can't make the world "OK" for them. Then, these destructive, ambivalent attitudes may be replayed in their object relationships later on in life.

Overprotective parents are threatened by the idea that their child is in any way handicapped. But the denial of the child's emotional vulnerability does her a great disservice no matter how lovingly this is expressed. Placing the "blame" for her problems on the "insensitivity" of her teachers, or on the "unfairness" of the camp, or on the "jealousy" of her friends can create a sense of entitlement that leads only to frustration and failure. Overly empathic and overprotective therapists may fall into the same trap, and fail their patients by not setting appropriate limits.

Constructive Realism

Some parents are able to accept the fact of their child's emotional vulnerability and they adopt a realistic and constructive attitude. They do not deny that their child has a problem and they are committed to handling this actively and constructively. They are not threatened, they do not lament, they do not overreact, they do not withdraw. They are able to love their anxious children not for what they want them to be, but for what they are in reality. They give their children the message that they will simply have to live with more anxiety than most of us, but unless they learn to accept this and do the best they can despite their difficulty, they will miss a lot in life. These children are discouraged from being angry and feeling sorry for themselves. Instead, they are encouraged to address their problems actively and constructively.

The fortunate individuals who were brought up with these healthy attitudes experience just as much panic and discomfort during a panic attack and get just as anxious and apprehensive in anticipation as others with this predisposition, yet they do not permit their handicap to get the best of them. These individuals have learned to be their own therapists. They limit their avoidances to the bare minimum. When they find themselves irrationally anxious, they make it a point to confront their terrors and they desensitize themselves. "I'm not going to let my ridiculous anxiety about rejection stop me from dating." They care about themselves and take pride in their ability to overcome their anxieties.

It should go without saying that the three patterns described above—parental rejection, overprotection, and constructive realism—are rarely seen in pure form. Most patients, while falling predominantly into one of the three categories, present a mixed picture, adapting well in some areas and avoiding others to their disadvantage.

The patient who comes for help for his sexual panics with constructive coping mechanisms is at a great advantage. But many patients we see in clinical practice present with long-standing maladaptive attitudes which pose an obstacle to the treatment process.

With these individuals we adopt a therapeutic stance comparable to that of realistic and constructive parents. We attempt to help them overcome their detrimental avoidance behavior and learn more constructive attitudes towards their fears. These issues complicate the treatment process, but can also extend the benefits of therapy beyond the relief of the sexual symptom to improvements in the other areas of life that the patient has avoided because of his panics.

SEPARATION ANXIETY

According to Klein (1980), pathologically prolonged and excessive separation anxiety is a cardinal feature of phobic anxiety syndrome. He further postulates that the separation anxiety experienced by patients with panic disorder is the product of a biological predisposition and is qualitatively different from that seen in other forms of psychopathology.

Our observations support this theory. We also find that problems related to separation anxiety are common sources of difficulty for our patients with panic disorders and sexual dysfunctions, and in many cases this tendency can be traced to childhood. The majority have histories of childhood difficulties with separations. In their adult relationships, many of our patients with sexual panic states clearly experience excessive *separation anxiety*. They also tend to overreact to *rejections and criticisms* from their lovers, and to take any sign of disapproval as a threat to the relationship.*

Of course, separation problems also occur in patients without panic disorders. Neurotic patients and patients with dependent, narcissistic, and borderline personality disorders often have problems with attachments and separations. In addition, they may lack the capacity for sustained, loving, committed romantic relationships. When such pathological object relationships develop in persons with biologically normal anxiety mechanisms because of traumatic events in their early development, there is no reason to believe that medication would be helpful. But some of our patients with sexual problems and phobic-anxiety syndrome are perfectly capable of forming mature, intimate, committed love relationships although they clearly have separation problems.

The clinical manifestations of related problems of adult separation

---

*The term "rejection sensitivity" has been used by Klein and others in connection with an interesting syndrome, "atypical depression." The essential feature of this disorder is that rejection by a lover precipitates severe clinical depressions that frequently lead to suicide attempts and/or hospitalizations. Atypical depression has an excellent response to MAOIs but not to TCAs, while patients with panic disorder respond both to MAOIs and TCAs (Quitkin et al., 1983: Quitkin et al., 1984; Liebowitz et al., 1984). The term "rejection sensitivity" is used here in a different sense to mean that the person overreacts to slight rejections or distorts situations that are not really rejections, and feels inappropriately hurt by these. In our experience there is a high correlation between overreactions to separations and rejections and I consider excessive sensitivity to rejection to be a manifestation of separation anxiety.

anxiety that are seen in patients with sexual disorders fall into two patterns. Some individuals with separation problems express their need for closeness by developing overly intense and dependent attachments, while others attempt to protect themselves from exposing themselves to pain by phobically avoiding love and commitment.

Panicky individuals who form these symbiotic attachments cannot love without fear. They tend to remain obsessively insecure with their partner and seek constant proof of love. Unless the spouse is exceptionally reassuring, they remain anxious and apprehensive, which may eventually repel the partner.

These individuals tend to become tense and insecure prior to separations and also before coming together again. For example, such a couple have fights before he leaves for a business trip or before she visits her mother, and they also tend to become tense and defensive when the spouse returns at the prospect of the wife making herself vulnerable once again. Individuals with separation problems tend to overreact and to feel personally rejected, angry, and depressed when the partner's commitment to work or avocation takes him or her emotionally away, even if this is temporary and clearly appropriate.

These individuals often obsess about their partner's sexual response, interpreting anything less than total abandonment and full responsiveness as a personal rejection or as a sign of their own sexual failure. These are the husbands who complain bitterly about their wives' coital anorgasmia, insisting that if she really found him attractive, his penis would "be enough" to give her an orgasm and she wouldn't "need" clitoral stimulation. And these women panic if their husbands should ejaculate rapidly or lose their erections, taking these as signs of rejection, but their anxious demands for a high level of sexual performance usually make things worse.

These separation-sensitive individuals can be at once pitifully vulnerable and tyrannically demanding, especially if they were raised in an overprotective family environment that taught them to expect and to feel entitled to unilateral and complete consideration. The combination of their vulnerability and these childhood experiences leaves these individuals with the distortion that anything less than perfect devotion is a rejection. They can become brutally hostile when they sense that they are not receiving the partner's total acceptance, and a sexual refusal can be the occasion of a major crisis.

The pressure for sexual performance exerted by partners with severe separation problems and hypersensitivity to rejection often constitutes the essential and immediate cause of the partner's sexual aversion. The sexually asymptomatic partner's anxiety becomes the crucial issue in treatment. The case of Grace and Gino (#17, p. 146) illustrates the role of the phobically anxious partner's sexual pressure in sexual aversion disorders and describes our therapeutic approach to this problem.

The sexual fate of persons who suffer from panic disorder-related separation problems will depend, to a large extent, on the emotional fit they work out with the partner. In order to feel the emotional security they need to function sexually, these sensitive souls need a close, intimate union with a lover who can handle their overreaction to rejection. If they connect with an ambivalent or rejecting or immature or sadistic partner, the relationship is likely to be one where they torture each other. But individuals with separation problems find it difficult to extricate themselves from relationships even if these are painful, and the couple may find themselves locked into a lifetime of marital hell.

However, with a giving, constructive, and sensitive person who finds the role of "good parent" egosyntonic and gratifying, these individuals can be wonderful partners and these couples can enjoy close, enduring, romantic, sexually gratifying relationships.

Other individuals with separation anxiety develop reaction formations against their wish for symbiotic closeness with the "ideal parent." Instead of clinging to their lovers, they develop "emotional claustrophobia." They panic at the idea of allowing themselves to become attached and protect themselves by avoiding emotional commitments. As much as they wish to be close to someone on one level, they also dread becoming vulnerable and dependent. They abhor the extent to which they can potentially feel controlled by their lovers. These defended individuals tend to develop sexual aversions when a relationship gets too close and they are heavily represented among those with aversion disorders secondary to marriage phobias.

When and if such avoidant individuals do on occasion drop their defenses and allow themselves to fall in love, they may do so with a painful, obsessive intensity. Not uncommonly, this rapidly turns into an aversion once again if they should succeed in winning the affections of the object of their desire.

The triad of separation anxiety, oversensitivity to rejection, and intolerance to criticism frequently plays a significant part in the genesis and maintenance of sexual aversions and of ISD. The couple's aspects of sex therapy often focus on these issues. This topic is discussed more fully in Chapter 6 on the treatment of the couple with sexual panic states.

CHAPTER 3

Etiology:
A Pluralistic Concept

Behaviorists, psychoanalysts, and psychopharmacologists have all attempted to treat and to conceptualize phobias and anxiety states. The three disciplines offer strikingly different hypotheses about the etiology and the psychopathology of these disorders. Not one of these models adequately accounts for the phobic phenomenon in its entirety, but each has clarified an important aspect.

THE LEARNING THEORY CONCEPT OF PHOBIC STATES

Behavior therapists and learning theorists have been interested in phobias since the great behaviorist Dr. James Watson and his colleagues treated children with animal phobias with methods derived from learning theory (Watson & Rayner, 1920; Jones, 1924).

In 1920 Watson described how he cured a little boy, Peter, of his intense fear of rabbits by gradually exposing him to the animal. First the rabbit was placed in the far corner of the laboratory, while the child was reassured, comforted, and fed a delicious lunch. When Peter learned to tolerate the rabbit in the corner, it was moved progressively closer. Soon the boy became so comfortable that he would munch nonchalantly with the animal perched on his desk. It was a historic moment. A phobia had been cured by systematically exposing the phobic individual to the previously avoided phobic object under pleasant and reassuring circumstances. At this writing 65 years later, these techniques which would later be termed *in vivo desensitization* and *reciprocal inhibition* still constitute the cornerstones of the behavioral treatment of sexual and other phobic symptoms.

Modern learning theories are based on two major concepts, each of which has given rise to specific treatment methods: *conditioning,* first discovered by Pavlov in the late 1800s, and *reinforcement,* which is based on the work of Skinner and his colleagues at the beginning of this century. *Two-factor theory* is a more recent development. This approach integrates both concepts to explain the acquisition and maintenance of pathological behavior and combines conditioning and reinforcement techniques in treatment. (Mowrer, 1939, 1974, 1950; Dollard & Miller, 1950).

According to *conditioning theory,* individuals learn to fear previously neutral objects or situations because the temporal association between that object (the conditioned stimulus) and situations which already evoke fear (the unconditioned stimulus) links the two experiences. For example, little Peter presumably acquired his rabbit phobia because a furry animal, perhaps a dog, which was originally a neutral stimulus, once actually frightened or hurt him, or because the mental image of a furry animal became associated in his mind with danger, perhaps because of a frightening story or witnessing an animal attacking someone.

From an evolutionary perspective, the capacity to form associations between previously disconnected experiences is a highly useful adaptive mechanism which allows us to be "programmed" to avoid dangerous situations—"the burned child doesn't touch fire." A conditioned avoidance response becomes a liability only if it persists when it is no longer useful. Thus, in traditional families young women are strongly encouraged to remain chaste while they are single. This is well and good until they get married. A young bride from a culture with severe prohibitions against premarital sex will experience problems if she is unable to alter her learned sexual avoidance after the wedding.

The ability to modify or discard a no longer useful learned response is obviously advantageous for creatures who must adapt to constantly changing environments. Our brain's capacity for continual "reprogramming" provides us with a flexibility without which we would be stuck with and heavily burdened by every learned response we have acquired throughout our lives.

Conditioning theory tells us that a learned response is erased or extinguished by reversing the conditioning process. The acquired response will gradually disappear when the feared object is repeatedly experienced in a nonpunishing or neutral context, or in temporal association with a pleasurable or rewarding state. In the language of learning theory, if the phobic child is repeatedly exposed to a rabbit which never bites, his fear response will eventually diminish by the process of *extinction*. If the rabbit is presented together with a tasty lunch and love, new positive responses will be acquired which will *reciprocally inhibit* and replace the unwanted fear reaction.

While the principles of conditioning explain the acquisition of a phobia, they do not account for its persistence or maintenance despite its painful consequences. But reinforcement theory offers an excellent explanation. According to that model, maladaptive responses are maintained and persist, even though they are ultimately painful, because of a self-perpetuating cycle of avoidance and reinforcement of the avoidance behavior. Skinner proposed that if an act is followed by or is instrumental in securing a reward, it will be learned and reinforced, while behaviors with painful consequences are likely to be extinguished or "unlearned" (Skinner, 1953). According to reinforcement theory, phobic individuals have learned to anticipate feared situations with apprehension and therefore have a compelling urge to avoid these. Their avoidance behavior is reinforced and maintained by the relief they feel when they manage to escape from an uncomfortable situation. In the language of learning theory, the unpleasant anticipatory anxiety that the phobic individual feels when he encounters the feared situation is a *secondary drive state* and behavior that is instrumental in its reduction becomes strongly reinforced and established. And if a person *avoids* his phobic object, extinction cannot take place and the phobic symptom is therefore maintained even though it is ultimately destructive to the individual.

For example, the sexaphobic patient who receives a sexual invitation will become anxious and feel a compelling urge to avoid this. He feels intense relief when he manages to make his exit, and the relief this affords, i.e. the reduction of his anticipatory anxiety, strongly reinforces his avoidance behavior so that it becomes deeply ingrained. The avoidance of dates and dances and frank sexual opportunities becomes a habit that is difficult to break, although this precludes corrective experiences and the ultimate consequences can be devastating.

In treatment, the patient's avoidance of the feared sexual situation is an absolute obstacle to the extinction of his inappropriate fears of sex. For these reasons, the relentless interference with the avoidance component of sexual panic states is one of the major strategies of the treatment of these patients.

According to learning theories, sexual phobias are acquired because of the simultaneous occurrence of sex and pain, which links the two experiences through the process of "sensory-sensory integration" within the central nervous system. Learning theory differs with the fundamental psychoanalytic contention that the association between sex and fear which causes sexual symptoms in adults is always established in early childhood during the Oedipal period. The notion that patients may acquire their sexual fears in childhood is not by itself at odds with learning theory. However, behaviorally oriented clinicians contend that the linkage between anxiety and sex can occur at any age. For example, sexual anxiety and avoidance are frequently acquired by *middle aged* persons who cannot handle the sexual slowdown that is part of the aging process. *Adolescence* is also a particularly sensitive period of sexual development, a time of high risk for acquiring sexual panic reactions.

Behaviorists tend to attribute the origins of sexual fears and conflicts more to cultural factors than to specific pathological family interactions. According to conditioning theory, sexual anxiety and guilt about sexual pleasure is acquired by many youngsters by the gradual process of assimilating the family's repetitive negative sexual "messages." In some cases, negative sexual conditioning occurs as a consequence of rape, incest, humiliating sexual failures, and painful disappointments in love.

Another major point of difference between the behavioral and psychoanalytic schools of thought is the contention of behavior therapists that sexual symptoms can be extinguished, irrespective of when and how they were acquired, *only* by the systematic exposure of the patient to the phobically avoided sexual situation under neutral and/or rewarding conditions. This is the basic strategy of the behavioral aspect of treatment of sexual phobias. According to this theory, delving into the patient's childhood makes no sense. In sharp contrast, the psychoanalytic position holds that *only* insight into and resolution of the patient's unconscious infantile sexual conflicts can cure his sexual panic state.

THE PSYCHODYNAMIC CONCEPT OF PHOBIC STATES

Psychoanalytic interest in phobias also began with the successful treatment of a little boy with an animal phobia (Freud, 1908/1966). In 1908, Sigmund Freud was consulted by colleagues about their son Hans, a five-year-old boy who had developed a phobic avoidance of horses. Since, at the turn of the century, Viennese streets and parks were crowded with horses, the child's phobia resulted in no small inconvenience for the household. Within the context of the foregoing discussion on extinction, the interesting point of this case is that the boy was cured of his phobia without ever having been exposed to or desensitized to horses and without any mention of horses or animals of any kind.

According to psychoanalytic theory, phobic anxiety is mobilized in patients with unresolved Oedipal conflicts when they repress their real concerns and displace their fears upon a neutral object. Freud believed that Hans was not really afraid of horses. He considered the boy's animal phobia symbolic for his real but unconscious fears of being castrated by his father and abandoned by his mother as punishment for his forbidden sexual and aggressive wishes. The treatment dealt only with these issues.*

The psychoanalytic theory of psychosexual development holds that all little boys between the age of four and five, when sexual feelings first begin to emerge, go through what is called the Oedipal phase of development, during which they want sex with their mother but fear retaliation from their father in the form of castration. Most children from stable homes with loving parents resolve their Oedipal conflicts without psychic damage. Others with less fortunate family situations find this difficult and develop neurotic symptoms.

In little Hans' case, there might have been some reality to the Oedipal hypothesis. The boy's mother was extremely beautiful and apparently seductive, which makes the idea that he was attracted to her plausible. The fear of punishment may have seemed very real to the boy since he had been literally threatened with castration for masturbating: "The doctor will cut off your widdler," and with banishment: "We will send you away."

Freud believed that the boy's fear of having his "widdler" cut off because of his ardent sexual longing for his beautiful mother, along with his jealousy of and rage towards his "rival," his father, produced intolerable inner conflicts. Freud further hypothesized that the child attempted to deal with these conflicts by repressing his real and dangerous incestuous wishes which he could not avoid, and displacing his fears onto an external object, a horse, which he could avoid more easily. It is much simpler for an immature ego to deal with a horse phobia than to face the dilemma created on the one hand by his strong sexual wishes and his competitive impulses and on the other by his fears of abandonment and castration.

Freud was, of course, far too astute a clinician to interpret Oedipal material directly to a five-year-old child. Instead, prompted by the assumptions described above, he advised the father to be more supportive and had the parents explicitly reassure the boy that they had no intentions of sending him away.

It was made clear to the boy that doctors do not cut off boys' widdlers and, in order to correct the confusing and frightening stories that Hans had received from his parents, in his only meeting with the boy Freud gave him simple and accurate information about sex and reproduction.

---

* Freud saw little Hans only on one occasion, but advised the father on management.

As a result of this brief, psychoanalytically oriented family intervention, the boy quickly lost his phobic avoidance of horses. It was a historic moment. A phobia had been cured with methods derived from Freud's theory of the unconscious which he had developed from his studies of hysteria.

This case illustrates the psychoanalytic view of phobias, and the psychodynamic treatment approach which in essence is still used today. According to modern psychoanalytic theory, neurotic persons who have not resolved their infantile Oedipal conflicts about sex and competition with their parents repress these into the realm of the unconscious where they lie dormant until the individual becomes sexually active. Later, as an adult, making love to a woman may activate the long-repressed incestuous wishes for his mother and the rivalry with his father, together with his castration anxiety. This mobilizes defenses against the dangerous impulse in order to prevent the "return of the repressed" or conscious recognition of the original dangerous Oedipal issues. According to this theory, the specific defense mechanisms involved in the pathogenesis of phobic disorders are *repression* of the Oedipal conflict and *displacement* of the fear onto the phobic object. Thus, the horse was avoided instead of the castrating father. In other cases the snake is avoided instead of the penis; food is avoided instead of fellatio; intimacy with the wife is avoided in place of incestuous closeness to mother; and a phobic woman may not be able to tolerate her husband's seeing her in the nude because she still can't face the guilt and pain of having tried and failed to seduce her father when she was a child.

Analytic theory holds that the phobic symptom always contains clues to the source of the patient's anxiety and also serves as a defense against this. For example, little Hans' phobic avoidance of horses kept him close at home with his secret love, his mother, but defended him against the conscious recognition of his incestuous wish and his fear of retaliation.

As another example of the dual, psychic meaning of the phobic symptom, the phobic avoidance of penetration might be conceptualized as the patient's defense against the conscious recognition of her repressed Oedipal wishes, and at the same as a symbolic expression of her refusal, by preserving her virginity for her father, to give up her struggle with her mother.

According to a psychoanalytic conceptualization, patients with sexual phobias and aversions are still struggling with their old Oedipal wishes. They fear and avoid sex because they make parent transferences towards their current sexual partners; thus, sex is, on an unconscious level, an incestuous act. Psychoanalytic theory predicts that when a patient resolves Oedipal conflicts and gains insight into the unconscious meaning of the phobic symptom, he or she will recover. The psychoanalytic therapies are designed to implement these objectives. According to this view, the patient does not really fear the phobic object and therefore the attempts to modify phobic symptoms directly with behavioral techniques makes no sense.

What would have happened if little Hans had been systematically exposed to horses while eating a piece of delicious Sacher Torte? Or to little Peter's rabbit phobia if he were reassured that his father would not hurt him and his mother would not abandon him? Would they have been cured? Probably. In retrospect it would appear that little Hans and little Peter both suffered from simple animal phobias, which we now believe respond well to a variety of psychological interventions. But it is interesting to speculate what would have happened had the boys been afflicted with phobic anxiety syndrome. They might have panicked during their treatments and it is entirely possible that neither Watson's nor Freud's therapies would have succeeded.

THE NEW BIOLOGICAL THEORY OF PHOBIC ANXIETY STATES

In the sixties Donald Klein discovered a fascinating group of highly anxious and phobic individuals who failed to respond to insight or behavior therapy and who were also refractory to the major and minor tranquilizers (Klein, 1964; Klein, 1980). He found that approximately 85 percent of these panicky individuals show a dramatic improvement with TCAs. These findings have been confirmed with double-blind studies by numerous investigators (e.g. Roth & Meyers, 1969). Subsequently, it has been shown that MAOIs and some of the newer antidepressant drugs, e.g. aprazolam, have similar antipanic effects (Klein, 1964; Sheehan et al., 1980; Zitrin et al., 1978).

Klein has hypothesized that the anxiety experienced by these patients is qualitatively different from the anxiety that is associated with neurotic processes; he called this drug-responsive disorder "Phobic Anxiety Syndrome." Klein proposed an interesting hypothesis to account for these clinical observations. He postulated that patients with Phobic Anxiety Syndrome suffer from a constitutional, biological abnormality in the form of a defective or malfunctioning CNS anxiety-regulating mechanism. More specifically, Klein hypothesized that individuals with Phobic Anxiety Syndrome are afflicted with an abnormally low physiological threshold for the alarm response, which causes them to experience excessive and inappropriate fears (panics) and predisposes them to develop phobias.

According to Klein's theory, panic disorder represents an abnormal continuation into adult life of the protest phase of the separation response.* This instinctual response causes newborn chicks, tiny kittens and other vulnerable neonates, including human babies, to squeal in distress when separated from mother and in turn sends the mother scurrying to take care of them. In normal individuals, the alarm-regulating center becomes adjusted to progressively lower levels as the individual matures, enabling him to tolerate separation from mother figures and later separation from others to whom he has formed attachments without undue discomfort. However, in patients with panic disorder, a residual excessive intolerance to separation is retained into adult life.

Several lines of observation support a link between panic disorder and separation anxiety. Real or symbolic loss of a significant relationship has frequently been reported as a precipitant of the disorder. Patients with panic disorder frequently have a history of school avoidance and other childhood difficulties with separations. Moreover, separation problems are highly prevalent among the children of patients with panic disorders (Weissman et al., 1984).

Biological regulatory mechanisms are known both to vary constitutionally and to exhibit vulnerability to external modification. The efficacy of antidepressants in blocking panic may lie in their ability to raise the threshold of the CNS mechanism that controls separation anxiety. Scott's finding that imipramine reduces separation-induced stress vocalizations in puppies (Scott et al., 1973) supports this hypothesis, as do Gittelman-Klein's studies which demonstrate the effectiveness of imipramine in children with separation anxiety (Gittelman-Klein & Klein, 1980).

Separation anxiety played a significant role in the psychopathology of a number of our patients with sexual panic states. On occasion, we observed a striking improvement of the couple's separation anxiety related difficulties after the panicky partner was medicated. We attribute many of the benefits of combined treatment to the reduction of pathological separation anxiety on the theory that, at least in some cases, this was related to the effects of the drugs.

---

* Bowlby (1973) has conceptualized separation anxiety as an innate response of the infant to the experience of separation from the home, nest, or mothering figure. He observed a three-step sequential response of the infant to separation—protest, despair, and detachment. The protest phase functions as a built-in (unlearned) early warning alarm system for recall of the parent. It may be speculated that the protest reaction in the early stages of the separation response has an adaptive value preventing irrevocable abandonment and preserving the life of the infant.

Klein attributes the unprovoked panic attacks that patients who are afflicted with phobic anxiety experience to spontaneous physiological discharges of their anxiety-regulating mechanism. He went on to explain the clinical picture seen in many agoraphobics with panic disorder and also in patients with panic disorders exhibiting the clinical features of "anxiety neurosis" as being the outcome of a three-stage process: The experience of recurrent spontaneous panic attacks leads the patient into a state of constant anticipatory dread and to self-protection through the avoidance of situations that are associated with episodes of panic.

This biological conceptualization suggests that sexaphobics with panic disorder are not really afraid of sex, but fear panicking and losing control. This implies that it makes no sense to look for the unconscious roots of the sexual fears of these individuals because insight will not reduce their fears. It also suggests that it is equally futile to attempt to modify their sexual avoidance with behavioral techniques while they are still susceptible to panic attacks.

The concept of an inherited biological variation in the CNS fear-regulating apparatus makes sense from the perspective of behavioral evolution.

Anxiety or fear is a danger signal that alerts us to impending dangers and prepares us physiologically to cope with these. The fear response activates our mental alertness and also enhances our physical energies so that we are in the best position to fight, flee, play dead, or survive by deception, intimidation, hiding, or calling for help. Created to protect life itself, this emergency system has the highest physiological priority. When the "alarm" sounds, all other ongoing activities that can safely be interrupted such as resting, eating or making love are preempted and the individual's resources become available for coping with the immediate crisis. The fear-alarm response is so advantageous for survival that it is present in all higher animals that have survived and evolved on this planet since the last great extinction. Not surprisingly, we homo sapiens are equipped with the finest, most sophisticated biological security-panic system evolved to this date.

Human panic and separation anxiety have their roots in the first primitive alarm system that safeguarded and insured the survival of the first vertebrates. These ancient panic circuits are still operable in our brains, and the mindless, primitive panic we feel in response to threat will always remain an integral part of our psyches.

Much later, the alarm mechanism which originally evolved to protect *individual* creatures became adapted to guard the safety of the immature, vulnerable young of birds and mammals through elaboration into what is called the "maternal instinct" (although in many monogamous species fathers also become protective and responsive to their young). This *mother-child alarm system* is based on mutual and reciprocal separation anxiety. From that time on, creatures would become alarmed about and respond with panic to danger not only to themselves but to *others* to whom they were emotionally attached. Thus, our separation anxiety seems to have evolved along with our capacity for love, altruism, empathy, and all the other lovely traits that go along with forming affectionate bonds with others. This ancient, biological heritage has made us decent, caring, and sensitive to others—but also highly vulnerable to losses and separations.

The brain's vigilance or alarm system also protects the individual from *future* hazards by "rewarding" effective adaptive behavior with a bit of pleasure and discouraging the repetition of dangerous acts by "punishing" these with a jolt of anxiety. When danger strikes, the pain-alarm circuits become activated, creating the painful aversive sensations that we label fear, anxiety, terror, and panic. These unpleasant feelings persist until the danger is past and impel the individual to seek safety. At the same time they condition him not to expose himself to peril again. When the individual is safe once more, this same alarm-regulating system produces an "all clear" signal that is subjectively experienced as a release from tension and a sense of pleasure and relaxation. These highly rewarding sensations select and reinforce the behavioral "program" that was instrumental in avoiding.or overcoming the danger.

In phobic anxiety syndrome, the threshold of this neural alarm-regulating mechanism is abnormally low, with the result that it may discharge spontaneously, very much like the spontaneous seizures experienced by the epileptic with a low seizure threshold. In addition, these patients also tend to react excessively and inappropriately to minor dangers, false signals, and any hint of separation and rejection. This can create profound disturbances in the lives of afflicted individuals.

Perhaps the following analogy, which I frequently use when attempting to help panic patients and their partners develop a compassionate understanding of their problem, might help to illuminate the disturbing inner experience of these tormented individuals.

I explain to these patients that everyone needs an alarm system to protect from danger, but that theirs is too sensitive. I tell the patient or the couple:

A properly adjusted security system will sound the alarm when an intruder breaks through the window. But if it is adjusted incorrectly, it might sound when a cat slinks by and may even go off by itself, occasionally. The family living in this house will know little sleep or tranquility, never being certain about when the next shrill and upsetting false alarm will shatter the peace. Some persons like you (or your wife) have alarm centers with abnormally low panic thresholds which may discharge spontaneously and which cause you to overreact with terrifying panics to harmless situations. It is not easy to live in a constant state of apprehension, with your existence continually disrupted by unpredictable panics, and it is difficult to get on with your life when your energies are consumed by the effort to cope with this.

At the same time I try to instill a sense of pride in the patient's achievements, accomplished despite his handicap, and to enhance his image in his partner's eyes. I also take this opportunity to introduce the notion that it might be possible, with the help of medication, to correct the adjustment of his oversensitive "panic thermostat" to a more normal level of responsiveness.

It is not difficult to understand why phobic anxiety has survived the evolutionary elimination race. A low panic threshold with its high level of anxiety can be advantageous under certain circumstances. Perhaps these traits were selected because once in some dangerous time and place hominids faced highly competitive environments. A low panic threshold with its perpetual vigilant state and a high level of separation anxiety gave the individual an edge in his struggle for survival and increased the odds that his vulnerable and edible young would survive in a habitat populated by predators. Perhaps, during the persecutions of the diaspora, those apprehensive European Jews with a low panic threshold who phobically avoided any sign of an impending pogrom (or the Holocaust) and who obsessively overprotected their children lived to reproduce, while their calmer cousins perished.

However, here and now in our relatively non-predatory society, persons who are afflicted with an overactive alarm system are at a terrible disadvantage and carry a heavy emotional burden which predisposes them to sexual panic states and to other kinds of psychopathology as well.

INTEGRATION

Behaviorists who were treating sexual disorders prior to the era of integrated sex therapy had focused only on the currently operating, consciously perceived causes of their patients' sexual symptoms. Psychoanalysts, on the other hand, had concerned themselves exclusively with their patients' underlying and unconscious sexual conflicts and with the remote origins of these in childhood.

In reality, currently operating sources of sexual anxiety and deeper emotional conflicts are equally important in the etiology of sexual disorders. This realization led to the development of the integrated sex therapy approach which espouses a pluralistic concept of etiology.

The integration of behavioral and psychodynamic theory has advanced and deepened our understanding of psychosexual disorders and the combined use of both techniques has improved our treatment capability substantially. We have now arrived at the point where we have a sound multidimensional model of the etiology of sexual phobias and aversion disorders in patients who have a normal capacity for anxiety, and we can intervene effectively at behavioral, psychodynamic, and/or relationship levels, as required in each particular case.

However, neither psychoanalysis nor theories of learning nor the integrated sex therapy approaches have until now adequately considered physiological variables in their formulations of psychopathology. As a result, we have not done well with patients with panic disorder. All of us, analysts and behavior therapists and also the "new sex therapists," have been making the error of assuming that all human beings are born equal with respect to their innate emotional make-up. We have all been mistaken in attributing the differences in the capacity for anxiety which we see in our patients solely to psychological or experiential determinants. But whether or not Klein's specific hypothesis will ultimately be proven correct, it is becoming increasingly evident that significant individual differences in the constitutional capacity for emotional responsiveness exist (Thomas & Chess, 1977) and I submit that these are important in the pathogenesis of certain sexual panic and phobic states. It was probably our failure to consider such constitutional factors which resulted in our inability to explain why some patients with sexual panic states remained irrationally fearful of sex, even though they had apparently attained valid insights into their unconscious sexual conflicts and even though they had conscientiously undergone extinction programs that seemed correct from a behavioral perspective. The new biological concept of phobic anxiety provides an attractive explanation for these baffling treatment failures. This, together with the success of antipanic medication for patients with panic disorders, has created the need to reconceptualize the pathogenesis of sexual panic states.

The theoretical construct of an abnormally low panic threshold cannot by itself account for the pathogenesis of sexual panic states.

With the exception of a small number of patients who developed a phobic avoidance of sex simply because they had previously panicked in a sexual situation and therefore anticipated another attack, the etiology was much more complex in most of our cases. The sexual symptoms of patients with sexual panic disorders are usually the product of the interplay between the constitutional propensity to panic and the same kinds of cultural and psychodynamic and relationship stressors which cause sexual problems in patients with a normal capacity for anxiety.

With the assumption that the concept of phobic anxiety syndrome is valid, it must be remembered that, while panic attacks may not surface as a clinical disorder until adult life, many if not all individuals with this syndrome are emotionally vulnerable from early childhood on, when most sexual conflicts and guilts are believed to originate. These anxious, sensitive individuals are probably even more likely to develop sexual guilt, neurotic conflicts, and marital problems than those who are biologically normal.

Biologically normal individuals and those with underlying panic disorders acquire their sexual fears by the same learning processes. But youngsters with low panic thresholds are much more likely to be traumatized by the negative sexual associations which most persons in our society experience in the course of their psychosexual development.

These anxiety-prone individuals are raised in the same kinds of neurotic families that predispose constitutionally normal children to neurotic problems. However, destructive home environments probably leave them with deeper scars. Psychological stressors are probably even more destructive to these defenseless youngsters and probably affect their psychosocial development and their sexual functioning even more profoundly. For these reasons psychodynamic issues must not be neglected when the diagnosis of panic disorder is made, but if anything should be considered even more meticulously when the patient has a biological vulnerability.

BEHAVIORISM AND THE NEW BIOLOGICAL THEORY OF ANXIETY

The laws of learning theory have not changed and the concepts of reinforcement and conditioning are no less valid because we now have additional data and a new biological theory of anxiety. Yet the behavioral formulations of sexual disorders will have to accommodate the possibility that a biological propensity for anxiety is material in the pathogenesis of certain sexual panic states and that medication is indicated for some of these patients.

In the language of learning theory, individuals who have a constitutionally low panic threshold can be expected to acquire sexual fear responses more rapidly, might tend to generalize these more widely to inappropriate situations, and might have negative associations linking fear with sex that would probably be more resistant to modification in these individuals.

For example, we have seen several individuals with phobic anxiety syndrome who developed a severe and persistent performance panic and a phobic avoidance of sex after a single sexual failure or trauma. This was illustrated in Case Vignette #5, of Mr. D. (p. 24). Ten years prior to his evaluation by us, this phobically anxious patient failed to achieve an erection and ejaculated rapidly during his first sexual attempt. He was 19 years old at the time. Already apprehensive about his ability to perform, he was so traumatized by this failure that he avoided sexual experiences entirely for the next 10 years. He was unable to approach women even when he dulled his terror with alcohol, and he eventually became suicidal.

A single episode that links sex with failure does not usually have such long-lasting and devastating consequences. Far more often when the sexual reflexes don't work all that well the first time, a person will try it again despite his apprehensions. But sexual trauma of any kind— punishment, failure, rape, or painful sex—is far more likely to result in a protracted sexual avoidance when the person to whom this happens is psychologically damaged or if he suffers from panic disorder.

CULTURAL CONDITIONING AND SEXUAL PANIC STATES

It was Masters & Johnson (1966) who first called our attention to the important role that cultural attitudes which link the natural biological function of sex with negative connotations of sin and shame play in the etiology of psychosexual problems.

The Judeo-Christian faiths fundamentally take the position that sex should be limited to married couples for the purpose of procreation. All other sexual practices are regarded as sinful and immoral.

More specifically, Orthodox Jewish and Roman Catholic law prohibits all sexual expressions except coitus between husband and wife for the purpose of procreation. Extramarital sex, premarital sex, contraception, masturbation, sexual fantasy, oral sex, and anal sex, homosexuality, and all variant sexual behavior or thoughts are defined as sins against God. Even within marriage, sexual practices that are conducive to intense erotic passion or "lust" are proscribed.

For example, lest sex be "immodest," Orthodox Jewish husbands are not allowed to look at their wives' genitals and must make love in the dark, preferably under the sheets. Orthodox Jewish men and women may not physically touch any adult person of the opposite sex except their own spouse (and this is allowed only at certain times). Thus, women and men may not shake hands and at festivities such as weddings men dance with men and women with women, separated by a screen and sharing only the sounds of the music.*

Boys from Orthodox Jewish homes receive strict prohibitions against masturbating and sexual fantasies. From the time they enter parochial school (Yeshiva) at the age of five, these youngsters are taught to suppress their erotic thoughts and to replace these with prayer and study. Boys and girls have no social or physical contact with one another until they are ready to marry.

The sexual values taught to children in devout Roman Catholic homes are nearly as restrictive. Catholic youngsters are also told from earliest childhood on that it is a mortal sin to masturbate and that erotic pleasure, thoughts, and feelings are "impure." Beginning in first grade, the nuns at parochial schools issue strict warnings to their little girls against tempting boys sexually. They are forbidden to use lipstick and advised not to wear patent leather shoes lest their shiny surfaces reflect the forbidden view under their skirts. The church encourages sexual continence by teaching Catholic children to fear eternal damnation should they give in to sexual temptation. They are required to confess and do penance for even minor lapses.

Although only a small fraction of the population observes these stringent sexual rules, Judeo-Christian moralistic values are deeply ingrained in our society. Even children raised in families who do not belong to fundamentalist religious groups seldom escape the sense that there is something wrong and shameful about sex. Even if sex is never mentioned explicitly, these youngsters get the clear message that sex is bad and that decent people have better things to think about.

Parents who think of themselves as liberal may voice enlightened views, but their deeper negative sexual attitudes are transmitted by their subtle, nonverbal, negative responses to a child's expression of sexual interest or pleasure. A youngster's sex education begins when he senses his mother's voice assuming a slightly harsher note and her movements becoming tense as she notices his erection in the tub. It becomes crystal clear to the perceptive child that his sexual feelings are definitely not okay.

---

* When we conduct sex therapy with Orthodox Jewish or devout Christian couples, we modify the behavioral aspects of treatment as far as this is possible so that the process of treatment does not conflict with their religious beliefs. For example, we do our best to avoid assignments that call for "spilling seed" (male masturbation), and we limit fantasy to erotic images that involve the patient's own spouse in order not to violate the commandment against adultery.

In our sexually ambivalent society, such negative associations are likely to be repeated on countless occasions, which leaves few of us entirely free of sexual conflict. However, the great majority, including most of those brought up in highly traditional and devout homes, end up functioning more or less normally as adults. But it is much more difficult for individuals who have significant emotional problems of psychogenic origin and also for those who are constitutionally vulnerable to anxiety to overcome their early negative training and they are at greater risk for developing sexual problems later on.

Parental admonitions against masturbation are bound to create some degree of conflict in all children, but Kinsey's finding that 98% of American males have masturbated (Kinsey, Pomeroy & Martin, 1948) and also the histories of numerous men from Orthodox Jewish and devout Christian homes who masturbated despite the strictest warnings attest to the fact that the effects of prohibitions against "self abuse" are usually temporary.

Most boys forbidden to masturbate will avoid doing so for a brief time only. The relief from sexual tension and the intense pleasure of orgasm serve to "reciprocally inhibit" the boy's recently learned avoidance of masturbation. He may be left with some residual sexual conflicts and guilts, but these tend to be relatively benign and temporary in normal youngsters. Most overcome the negative effects of childhood prohibitions against masturbation entirely by the time they become sexually active.

But a child who has a low panic threshold and who may be handicapped by excessive separation anxiety is likely to be far more sensitive and responsive to parental censure. The malignant synergism between restrictive sexual training and the child's constitutional vulnerability is seen in the greater damage often apparent in these vulnerable individuals. His mother's objections to masturbation, even when they are mild and tempered with love, carry the intensely alarming threat of maternal rejection and abandonment. It may, therefore, be too risky for the anxious, phobic child to disobey and these vulnerable youngsters can develop especially intense and damaging masturbation guilt and avoidance.

I have seen a number of cases of sexual avoidance that could be traced to a chain of events that began when childhood masturbatory inhibitions were overlearned and persisted into adult life. This is likely to happen because a child's special vulnerability makes him more impressionable, as well as on account of a sadistic parent's abusive punishments for masturbation.

The following case vignette illustrates some of the long-range destructive effects that masturbatory avoidance can produce in vulnerable individuals, even when they are raised in stable, loving, nurturing family environments.

Case Vignette #6: Mr. E.

The patient was a 65-year-old man who presented with a chief complaint of impotence, retarded ejaculation, and sexual avoidance of two years' duration. He had been married to his second wife, who was 57 years old, for five years.

The patient had never masturbated because he had heeded his father's warnings that masturbation and ejaculation would cause him to "lose the marrow out of his bones." This admonition grew out of the father's ignorance, as he was loving and encouraging to the boy in other respects.

The patient had a panic disorder with recurrent mild spontaneous panic attacks and mitral valve prolapse. Except for some separation-related problems with his wife, the patient was a highly successful, well functioning man who was not impaired by his panic disorder.

E. married for the first time when he was 21. His wife had been his only sexual partner, and during the initial 20 years of this marriage he had functioned with relatively little difficulty. However, his early sexual inhibition had left him with latent problems which made it difficult for him to maintain his sexual functioning when emotional problems arose with his first wife. These also impaired his ability to cope with the physical slowdown of sexual responsiveness that is part of the normal aging process.

This patient's first marriage began to deteriorate when he was in his late 40s and he found it progressively more difficult to ejaculate. He was too insecure sexually to seek other sexual partners, and his attempts to relieve his sexual tension with masturbation evoked the old inhibitions. Although he became aroused, he could not reach an ejaculation. These unsuccessful experiences left him physically uncomfortable and emotionally vulnerable.

He sought a divorce and married a woman to whom he was deeply attracted. In the beginning of this relationship he was again unable to ejaculate, but he was able to overcome this problem within a few months. For the next three years the couple had successful intercourse. Two years prior to the consultation, E.

began to experience episodes of erectile loss when he tried to "hold back" his orgasm until his wife climaxed, as he had been accustomed to doing. He felt demeaned and he became angry at her loving suggestion that he should try to ejaculate more rapidly and that she could have her orgasm with clitoral stimulation afterwards. Mr. E. had never been able to ejaculate except intravaginally during coitus, and he was frustrated and depressed by his inability to climax when she tried to stimulate him orally or manually.

Our medical work up revealed a borderline abnormality of his nocturnal erections and indicated that his penile circulation was mildly impaired.

Most men can accommodate to such minor age-related changes in their sexual capacity by increasing their psychic and genital stimulation. But Mr. E.'s old masturbatory inhibitions made this difficult for him. He had never learned to fantasize, and he could not respond to direct genital stimulation. Since intercourse was now a little difficult for him, he developed performance anxiety and functional difficulties and saw no recourse but to avoid sex.

Gender Specific Problems

Sexual messages are gender specific, and tend to create different sorts of problems for men and women. We train our girls for a supporting role in the bedroom, while the boys are expected to star. Women are therefore less likely to be handicapped by the performance pressures that plague their partners. Instead, they often develop sexual problems because they find it more difficult than men to assert themselves sexually.

Women so conditioned find it much easier to give than to receive sexual pleasure. This tendency is heightened in women with underlying panic disorders. Unless they feel totally secure in the relationship, these women tend to become obsessively overconcerned with fulfilling their partners' sexual desires. Their fears of rejection are assuaged only when they are certain they are satisfying their lovers. They are unable to focus on their own sexual needs or pleasures lest this interfere with the obsessive pursuit of the reassurance they obtain when their lovers respond. In sex therapy, women with this problem are threatened by and tend to resist assignments that call for them to step out of their "giving" roles and to express their own desires.

A brief description of the treatment of Frances, a young woman with anorgasmia and panic disorder, will illustrate the role of such compulsive "sexual sacrifice" in the etiology of sexual aversion.

Case Vignette #7: Frances

This 29-year-old, highly intelligent, attractive social worker was intensely distressed by her inability to experience orgasm.

The patient had never masturbated until she was advised by a friend one year before consulting us that this might help her have orgasms. During these attempts, she experienced palpitations and shortness of breath when she reached a high level of excitement, and would then stop stimulating herself.

Her urge to avoid sexual stimulation and arousal was even more compelling when she was with a partner.

This patient met the criteria for panic disorder. She reported several episodes of spontaneous panics and she also had other phobias. However, she was seen before we began using antipanic drugs in these cases and she was not medicated.

Frances grew up under emotionally difficult circumstances which contributed to her sexual problem. Frances's mother was extremely possessive and jealous of Frances's father, who was described as attractive, charming, and promiscuous. She worried obsessively that her husband would fall in love with another woman and leave her, and she did not hide her fears from her daughter. Throughout Frances's childhood and adolescence, the sensitive child had witnessed recurrent crises that centered around her father's infidelities and her mother's angry, despairing recriminations. Frances was determined to avoid her mother's helpless position and masochistic role with men, but at the same time she was drawn to her seductive father.

These family problems had left their mark and were reflected in the instability of Frances's romantic relationships. A bright, sensuous, charming young woman, she never failed to attract men. She had been involved in numerous romances, but these had never lasted more than a few months. Initially, she would feel enthusiastically infatuated with each new lover, but she invariably developed a sexual aversion as soon as he wanted more of a commitment from her. She would then use the unpleasant sexual experience as the excuse for ending the relationship.

Her current sexual experience was typical and revealing. She was "crazy" about Frank, her handsome 24-year-old medical student lover of three months. An echo of her mother, Frances was intensely jealous of Frank and she worried obsessively that he would leave her, although he gave her no reason to doubt his devotion.

When they made love, Frances stimulated and satisfied Frank, but would not allow him to reciprocate. At the time of her consultation she was just beginning to feel the old familiar resentment and she was concerned, with good reason, that she was about to lose her interest in this relationship, as she had always done in the past.

I attempted to extinguish Frances' panicky response to and phobic avoidance of receiving erotic stimulation, which was the immediate cause of her anorgasmia, and to accustom her to accepting stimulation from her partner. However, my suggestion that she allow Frank to pleasure her even briefly threatened to disrupt her compulsive defenses against her fears of abandonment and met with strong resistance. (The treatment of this case is described in Chapter 5.)

This vignette illustrates a common pathogenic process that can occur with women who find little pleasure in lovemaking because they are too anxious to ask or permit their partners to stimulate them. As they continue to provide gratification for their partners, while they manage to receive no pleasure for themselves, they eventually become resentful towards their lovers and develop secondary sexual aversions.

There is no sharp dividing line between the cultural and neurotic causes of sexual panic states. Neurotic patients who grow up in pathological family environments are more vulnerable to the deleterious effects of culturally transmitted negative attitudes, while emotionally disturbed individuals are likely to use the sexually restrictive teachings of their religion in the service of their neurotic avoidance of sex. But again, patients with panic disorders are more vulnerable to neurotic as well as to cultural stressors.

PSYCHOANALYSIS AND THE NEW BIOLOGICAL THEORY OF ANXIETY

The new biological discoveries have not diminished the value of the psychodynamic model for understanding and treating sexual anxiety states. Even though I do not accept many of the tenets of psychoanalysis, I continue to find certain key concepts extremely useful for conceptualizing the deeper dynamics of patients and couples with sexual panic states, and I consider the brief psychodynamic therapy techniques which are derivatives of psychoanalysis invaluable in the comprehensive treatment of these patients.

But psychoanalysis, like behaviorism, will have to accommodate the growing evidence that individual differences in the physiological capacity for anxiety could well have a heretofore unaccounted for and profound influence on psychosexual development and on the genesis of certain kinds of sexual anxiety states. And analysts will also have to come to grips with the possibility that some anxious patients might need medication.

According to psychoanalytic theory, a child's emotional experiences during the first five years of his life shape his personality and determine whether he is destined to enjoy psychological health or suffer emotional illness.

The psychoanalytic theory of psychosexual development divides these critical formative years into the oral, anal and Oedipal periods, and postulates that a child will develop a healthy personality and a normal romantic life only if he is able to master each of these three phases successfully. Furthermore, specific personality disorders, neurotic symptoms, relationship problems, and sexual difficulties are all thought to result from specific kinds of traumatic events and pathological interactions with family members during each of these phases.

A child's difficulties during these phases and the eventual emotional consequences have generally been attributed solely to the pathological dynamics of his family environment and to his parents' destructive attitudes towards him. Thus, we read about the role of "schizophrenogenic" families and "castrating" mothers in the etiology of various psychiatric disorders. But the constitutional vulnerability of the panic prone child, his low panic threshold, his separation anxiety, and his tendency to overreact to criticism and rejection are bound to influence and complicate the course of his psychosexual development. The ultimate outcome of this complicated sequence will depend to a great extent on the nature of his interactions with the members of his family.

The *oral period* marks the first two years of life when the child must establish a mutually affectionate and effective emotional bond with his mother if he is to survive and thrive. In his early writings, Freud advanced the hypothesis that traumatic experiences that occur during the oral period result in predilictions for oral sex, eating disorders, alcoholism, and other addictions, and also predispose the individual to depression. Some years later when psychoanalytic attention shifted to ego functions, it was further postulated that disturbances in the mother-infant bond also exert a destructive effect on ego development and impair the person's ability to love and form intimate committed romantic relationships. The pathogenesis of the more serious narcissistic and borderline personality disorders which are marked by disturbed object relationships was attributed to oral phase difficulties.

More specifically, according to Erikson (1968), the first year of life, the oral phase, is the critical period for the development of the "basic trust" of others, which constitutes the essential psychological foundation upon which the capacity to form caring and gratifying object relationships is built. Basic trust can develop only if the infant is able to establish a trusting, reliable, loving, and nonmanipulative relationship with her mother. In other words, the infant must know that she is safe with her mother and that she can count on her to love and take care of her, completely secure in the knowledge that she will never abandon her or do her harm. If the maternal-infant relationship lacks these qualities, for any reason, be it the mother's absence, her psychopathology, or family stresses, the individual's significant relationships are destined to be flawed and problematic for the rest of her life.

But if an infant has a constitutional propensity to panic and an excessive intolerance to separations, this delicate dyad could easily be disturbed. Wouldn't it be difficult for a child to develop a trusting relationship with his mother when his needs for her are so excessive that no matter how hard she tries, no matter how caring and loving she is, she simply cannot protect her anxious, vulnerable baby from feeling deprived and insecure at times. She can't possibly be there enough for him and right from the beginning he will begin to connect pain with love.

An important condition for good romantic relationships is that each is free to love the other without having to protect him/herself against the possibility of hurt or exploitation. But these babies may never have experienced love without separation anxiety, and their fears about being hurt in love and their defenses against closeness become an integral part of and disturb their object relationships.

This developmental period is even more hazardous when the vulnerable infant's mother has significant problems of her own which cause her to become overly merged with the infant or to reject him. These hypersensitive children are likely to sustain more damage from interactions with a disturbed mother who could not meet the emotional needs of any infant than those with a normal capacity to defend themselves.

It is a tribute to excellent parenting that some of these panicky, phobic individuals actually end up with healthy loving, caring, intimate relationships. However, difficulties in their romantic relationships are a serious problem for many patients with sexual panic states.

The *anal period,* which takes place between the ages of two and four, is dominated by the struggle between the parents and the child over his bowel control. Psychoanalytic theory contends that individuals who become fixated at the anal stage are left with unresolved rage and ambivalence and tend to develop obsessive-compulsive neuroses and personalities and sadomasochistic sexual interests.

Quite apart from the validity of these speculations, patients with phobic anxiety syndrome frequently develop obsessive-compulsive defenses and character traits in the attempt to deal with their anxieties. Some become obsessively concerned about their sexual performance and/or develop a compulsive need to please their partners. They become sexually dysfunctional for these reasons.

The *Oedipal period* takes place between the ages of four and five when sexual and romantic feelings for the parent of the opposite gender emerge. At the same time, the child enters into a competitive struggle with the same sex parent. This is regarded by psychoanalysts as the most imortant phase of psychosexual development with respect to the genesis of sexual symptoms, and the successful resolution of Oedipal conflicts is considered essential for normal adult psychosexual functioning. Sexual disorders, including phobias and aversions, are attributed to the child's difficulties in resolving the conflicts that arise during the Oedipal phase.

In order to succeed in this complex developmental task, the child must have not only the courage to compete with the same sex parent but also the emotional capacity to give up the struggle with good grace and to love his former adversary enough to forgive him. The child's ability to handle this triangle successfully has been attributed to how well he has done in his earlier development, to the structure of the family, and to his relationships with his parents. However, the child's constitutionally determined emotional make-up is also an important determinant which has not been given sufficient consideration.

If all goes well, boys do their best to win their mother's exclusive love, but they should eventually be able to give up when they see the hopelessness of their quest. Normal boys let go of their rage against their mother for "rejecting" them and their envy of their father for "winning." They are then able to form a healthy identification with their father which prepares them to ultimately find their own lover and to enjoy mature, gratifying heterosexual relationships.

In a similar but even more complex developmental sequence, the little girl must have the strength to challenge her mother's place with the father. Eventually, however, she too must relinquish her romantic attachment to her father. If she is to complete her feminine development, she must give up her vengeful fantasies toward her mother and form a close identification with her. If all these pieces fall into place correctly, women are then free to fall in love with an appropriate man and to enjoy vaginal orgasms.*

According to psychoanalytic theory, individuals who cannot give up their desires for their mothers or fathers, nor their struggles with the same sex parents, are destined to suffer from sexual problems and unhappy relationships, as well as from success conflicts all their lives.

I find the concept of the "Oedipal conflict" extremely useful in some cases, but not applicable to others. Freud's hypothesis that all psychosexual disorders can be traced to unresolved Oedipal problems is not supported by our experience. Many of our patients with sexual phobias and other dysfunctions show no evidence of such dynamics, and their problems can be traced to other causes. For example, the case of Bridget (Case Vignette #9, p. 100) illustrating female avoidance of intercourse was conceptualized as resulting from the interplay between her biological panic syndrome and culturally determined sexually restrictive attitudes. The case was successfully concluded without any reference to oedipal material.

However, we frequently do see patients whose sexual phobias and aversion can clearly be attributed to their mother transferences to their wives or father transferences to their husbands. Thus Frances' (p. 55) resistance to the modification of her anorgasmia and her problems with men were attributed, at least in part, to her reenactment, without her conscious awareness, of her Oedipal problems. A similar formulation also made sense in explaining B.'s attachment to his rejecting wife (Case Vignette #3, p. 20).

The sexual and romantic relationships of these neurotic individuals never seem to work out. On some unconscious level they still seem to be yearning for their parents. Men with unresolved Oedipal problems eventually become disappointed with and/or destructive towards each woman who becomes involved with them. Women with unresolved Oedipal problems have similar difficulties. Remaining fixated on their fathers, they are conflicted about committing themselves to appropriate men and remain ambivalent towards their partners. Men with unresolved Oedipal problems typically have no insight into the unconscious pro-

---

* Freud's assertion that clitoral eroticism is pathological has come in for a great deal of criticism in the last decades since the advent of the woman's movement. While I believe that politics should not compromise scientific integrity, clinical evidence apart from any feminist considerations clearly supports the contrary position. It is now the consensus of clinicians who work with sexual problems that clitoral eroticism and vaginal sensitivity are both normal aspects of female sexuality (DSM-III, 1980; Alzate, 1977). Approximately 75 percent of normal women require direct clitoral stimulation in order to climax. I consider the obsession for vaginal orgasm as a pathological manifestation on the part of the woman and/or her partner.

cesses that govern their lives and, unless therapy intervenes, may be doomed to perpetual cycles of ardently striving for and then sabotaging their sexual and romantic success. The formation of a sexual aversion towards the partner is a frequent expression of this destructive pattern.

Patients with unresolved Oedipal problems are also likely to develop success conflicts and anxiety about competition in the nonsexual aspects of their lives because "winning" is always Oedipal for them. When they win, they punish themselves. These individuals sometimes develop sexual difficulties as an unconscious "trade off" to "pay" for their career successes. This dynamic is frequently material in their sexual difficulties and may mobilize resistances to the behavioral modification of this sexual symptom.

How does the phobic anxious child deal with the Oedipal triangle? On the assumption that the Oedipal concept is valid, one would predict that this is a most hazardous period for these vulnerable youngsters.

It is often safer for a small boy who is anxious about being abandoned to back off from the competition for his mother's love when he senses his father's neurotic need to win every contest. And he is apt to play "the loser" for the rest of his life.

In another typical scenario, the urgent need to please his mother makes the anxious little boy particularly vulnerable to maternal seductiveness. The thoughtless mother's manipulations, which grow out of her own neurotic needs, are gratified by her son's attachment to her. But this might make it difficult for her vulnerable boy to separate himself from her and could set up a lifetime pattern of passivity and dependence on women.

And how can the vulnerable little girl risk approaching her father when her antennae tell her that her mother is too insecure to tolerate sharing the father's attention? It is easier to avoid the competition and let her win if that is the price for staying in her good graces. But when she is grown up, she is apt to continue to avoid competing for love and she will always let the "other woman" have the desirable man.

The excessive emotional dependency these phobically anxious little girls have on their mothers predisposes them to remain perpetually in an infantile, compliant, "good little girl" role. In an equally self-defeating pattern, they may rebel and engage in senseless destructive and vengeful competitions with other women for the rest of their lives.

The same kinds of pathological family interaction also lead to emotional and sexual problems in biologically normal individuals, but the symptoms of individuals with underlying panic disorders and separation anxiety tend to be especially severe and resistant to therapy.

RELATIONSHIP PROBLEMS AND SEXUAL PANIC STATES

No discussion about the etiology of sexual aversion disorders can be complete without considering the important role played by difficulties in the couple's relationship. Among Masters and Johnson's most important contributions to the field of sexuality was their recognition that a sexual inadequacy is often caused by the couple's inability to communicate and by partner rejection (Masters & Johnson, 1970). They protested against the shortsightedness of treating only the symptomatic patient, which was the accepted procedure at that time, by defining the "marital unit" as "the patient." They would not accept individuals without partners for treatment (Masters & Johnson, 1970).*

While there is no question about the validity of a dyadic approach to the treatment of sexual aversion disorders, a distinction must be made between the lesser role of relationship difficulties in *primary* as distinguished from *secondary* sexual aversion. Patients who have *always* avoided sex often have inner conflicts of such magnitude that these would surface with anyone.

In spite of this, the dynamics of the couple's relationship must be considered even in the primary forms of these syndromes because a destructive partner, although not implicated in its genesis, can play a significant role in *maintaining* the spouse's primary sexual aversion. And even when this is not the case, it is often advisable to conduct treatment conjointly because a cooperative partner can be invaluable in helping the symptomatic patient to overcome his or her avoidance.

However, destructive interactions in the couple's current relationship are often the major problem in cases where the patient's avoidance of sex developed after a period of normal functioning. In these *secondary aversion disorders,* the couple's troubled marital system often becomes the major focus of treatment.

Realistic and Neurotic Ambivalence

Occasionally, couples who love one another and are committed to their marriages develop sexual aversion and avoidance because of simple performance anxieties, inadequate sexual techniques, or the inability to communicate their sexual needs to one another effectively.

More often, the relationship problems of these couples are far more

---

* Because they believed that sex therapy should always be conducted conjointly, Masters & Johnson for a time provided single dysfunctional patients with surrogate sexual partners (Masters & Johnson, 1970).

complex. The avoidance of sexual difficulty is usually an expression of an unrecognized ambivalence towards the partner. It may be difficult for a person to admit that he has become unhappy with the relationship and avoidance of sex may be the first sign of the hidden marital problem.

In some cases the person becomes ambivalent because the relationship really does not work. For instance, a woman may become disillusioned about her marriage, and "turned off" sexually because of her growing awareness that she had overestimated her husband's intelligence and his potential and now finds herself "stuck" with a timid, passive man who does not share her ambitions. Or a wife's latent emotional problems surface after the wedding and the spouse finds that he is trying to build a life with a woman who is too depressed or too anxious to function.

At first the ambivalent partner may attempt to suppress the conscious recognition of his disappointment and try to make the best of it. But the individual's inner anger may break through in the form of an aversion to sex.

More often, however, in clinical practice we see individuals who are repelled by their spouses on account of *irrational distortions* and *neurotic processes* when there is no real reason to complain about the partner. Such irrational ambivalence can grow out of various types of pathological marital interactions.

A number of models have come out of the marital therapy literature which I find particulartly useful for conceptualizing the dynamics of couples who avoid sex and for implementing the goals of sexual therapy. These include the constructs of: neurotic power struggles, contractual disappointments, mutual childhood transferences, and neurotic fears of commitment and intimacy.

Unrecognized power struggles are often the source of chronic, smouldering marital rage and ambivalence which can result in sexual aversion. When a husband approaches his wife who is furious with him because he has won the last round in their struggle for control, she is apt to experience sensations of revulsion and anger and a compelling urge to avoid his touch, rather than erotic arousal.

The marital power struggles of individuals with pathological separation problems frequently center around the vulnerable partner's tendency to overreact to distance, rejection, and criticism, and his or her defenses against getting hurt. The panicky person has an intense need for his partner's commitment and closeness, and may experience even appropriate or temporary distance as a painful rejection. Bitter struggles can erupt if he should become absorbed in a business crisis or if she announces that she wants to enroll in graduate school.

Contractual disappointments (Sager et al., 1972) are another source of irrational marital ambivalence and anger. The spouse who feels shortchanged frequently develops an aversion to sex. Couples with panic disorders are not immune to contractual difficulties. Their conflicts often center around the anxious partner's unrecognized separation problems. The unexpressed marital "deal" that the anxious partner typically assumes he has made with his wife is that he has obligated himself to make every effort to gratify her needs, to take care of her, and to be a committed and faithful partner. In return he behaves as though she has promised that she will be unhesitantly available to him, always respond to his dependency needs, and never threaten, reject, or leave him. The biologically normal partner may unknowingly "welsh" on the deal, simply because she is not aware of her husband's expectations and also because she does not fathom the extent of his emotional vulnerability.

Individuals with panic disorder related separation problems are often bright, talented, competent, and successful, and it may be very difficult to discern their inner vulnerability. For this reason, the spouse who has made a sincere effort to be giving and considerate is apt to be puzzled and angered by her husband's rages, demands, and depressions. Neither may understand that he feels "gypped" because he is going out of his way to give her everything that she wants, but he is not getting the intense emotional closeness he needs and feels entitled to. This dynamic is illustrated in Case Vignette #12 on p. 115 which describes a struggle that centered around a sensitive husband's overreaction to his wife's commitment to her career.

Transference of unresolved Oedipal conflicts and sibling rivalry probably occurs to some degree in all marriages and love affairs. When mild, it is not pathological and may even lend energy and color to the relationship. But the neurotic transference of unresolved childhood issues can also be extremely destructive to the couple's marriage and to their sexual relationship.

The parental and sibling transferences that individuals with phobic anxiety syndrome make to their lovers tend to be especially intense and dramatic. Their separation fears fuel and intensify their possessiveness, their need to be the "favorite," and their infantile dependency needs. They tend to become obsessive in their demands, enraged when they are frustrated by their "wife-mothers" or their "husband-fathers," and demoniacal when they feel "bested" by their "siblings." The pressure they can exert may cause the *biologically normal partner* to develop a sexual aversion. The spouse is turned off on account of the obsessive partner's relentless jealousies and insecurities. If treatment is to succeed with such couples, it is the phobically anxious spouse and not the one with the sexual symptom who must develop insight and change his behavior.

The Fear of Intimacy and Commitment

Some patients develop an aversion to sex with their partner in the service of their defensive *avoidance of love, closeness,* and *commitment.* Patients with intimacy and commitment conflicts make love without difficulty during the beginning phases of a relationship, but develop "emotional claustrophobia" which frequently goes along with sexual aversions and the avoidance of sex when the partner demands a deeper level of commitment.

There are considerable individual differences in the tolerance level for emotional closeness. Normal individuals can meld erotic desire and intimacy and are able to enjoy a gratifying sexual relationship with the partners to whom they are committed. But the "emotional comfort zone" of a person with intimacy conflicts is exceeded at a certain point of increasing commitment. One individual may abruptly begin to lose his desire and/or avoid sex after an invitation to join the partner for a weekend trip, while another does not feel threatened until she wants an exclusive relationship or until they begin to live together. Persons with somewhat higher intimacy tolerances may remain sexually active until the engagement, the honeymoon, or the birth of a child, when they may "turn off" abruptly.

An emotional crisis is created when the level of closeness exceeds the patient's defensive threshold and taps into his latent fears of rejection and abandonment. He loses his sexual interest and/or begins to panic when he senses that he is becoming vulnerable and emotionally dependent on his partner. Patients with commitment and intimacy conflicts become ambivalent about the relationship on an irrational basis. They feel threatened and develop sexual aversions even though their partners may be caring and sensitive to their needs and there is no reality to their fear that they will get hurt.

Patients with panic disorder are especially likely to develop serious fears of intimacy and commitment. The avoidance of deep relationships as well as the split between erotic and intimate feelings often take on the dimensions of an "emotional claustrophobia" in these individuals. The psychosocial treatment approach to sexual panic states associated with this dynamic is discussed in Chapter 5.

PANIC DISORDER AND OTHER PSYCHOSEXUAL
DYSFUNCTIONS

Thirty-one percent of our patients with a phobic avoidance of sex also suffered from genital phase sexual dysfunctions. In some cases the patient's sexual avoidance was a consequence of and secondary to his inability to function; at other times the dysfunction was caused by the physiologic concomitants of the patient's panicky response to sex. The high coincidence between sexual panic states and dysfunctions is not surprising. Apprehension about sexual performance, obsessive self observation or "spectatoring," and overconcern with the partner are considered to be the three most common immediate or currently operative causes of the psychosexual dysfunctions (Masters & Johnson, 1970; Kaplan, 1974, 1979, 1983). These destructive mental processes are all apt to be heightened in patients with panic disorders.

An additional element in the pathogenesis of the sexual dysfunctions in these patients and a complicating factor in their treatment is their propensity for experiencing difficulties with their lovers because of their separation anxieties and their oversensitivity to rejection. Unless they feel especially close to and secure with their partners, men and women with phobic anxiety syndrome may find it extremely difficult to suspend their concern about satisfying their lovers and to abandon themselves to their erotic pleasure.

The anxiety generated when such individuals are insecure in their sexual relationship can interfere with their sexual desire and/or with the excitement and orgasm reflexes on a physiological basis. This predisposes them to functional difficulties. Often, what under ordinary circumstances would be a temporary, minor, dysfunctional episode can, in panic prone individuals as well as in those whose insecurities are based on neurotic conflicts, escalate into a downward spiraling cycle of anticipation of failure, panic, and avoidance. This can ultimately result in chronic sexual problems.

We have never found any specific differences in the underlying biological, cultural, interpersonal, and neurotic sources of the sexual anxiety that is involved in the pathogenesis of the different dysfunctional syndromes. For example, a deeply religious man who experiences sexual anxiety because he has been trained to suppress his sexual impulses throughout his childhood and adolescence is equally likely to develop retarded ejaculations, impotence, or inhibited sexual desire (ISD). This is also true of the individual with neurotic sexual anxiety. But the specific characteristics of the anxiety which is experienced in the current sexual situation and the individual's particular defenses against these constitute the "immediate causes" of the sexual dysfunction, and these are highly specific and different for each syndrome (Kaplan, 1974, 1979).

The manifestations of the person's sexual anxiety interfere with the sexual response cycle at different points. Therefore, orgasm phase disorders develop when sexual anxiety is experienced and defended against during the orgasm phase, while impotence results from excitement phase anxiety and ISD from apprehension prior to a sexual opportunity, when the person begins to feel pleasurable anticipation (Kaplan, 1974, 1979).

These same mechanisms are involved in the pathogenesis of the genital phase dysfunctions of patients who have a normal capacity for anxiety, as well as of those with panic disorder. But the intensity of the fear experienced by patients with panic disorders complicates the course of sexual dysfunctions and their treatment because their anticipatory anxiety predisposes them to avoid corrective sexual experiences in real life, and also to resist therapeutic sexual interactions during the course of sex therapy.

CHAPTER 4

Sexual Disorders and Medication

Donald F. Klein, M.D.

Patients whose chief complaints lie in the sexual sphere frequently have concomitant symptoms of anxiety and/or depression. These symptoms are often interpreted by the therapist as an understandable reaction to the distress of sexual incompetence or frustration. However, such an assumption is unwarranted without a detailed diagnostic assessment. The reasons are straightforward. Anxious and depressive disorders may directly *cause* sexual dysfunction and the alleviation of the sexual dysfunction may depend on their primary cure. Even if the sexual problem is not directly caused by the anxious or depressive states, these illnesses may well prevent the carrying out of effective therapeutic interventions. Therefore, their concurrent treatment may enhance sex therapy.

Recently, there has been a substantial increase in our knowledge concerning the differential diagnosis of the anxious and depressive states. This differential diagnosis is of practical value because it is now clear that illnesses that appear quite similar may, nonetheless, require different medications. The use of medication, however, is a two-edged sword. Although frequently invaluable and necessary for the alleviation of anxiety and depressive disorders, medication may actually produce sexual difficulties in some cases. Therefore, the alert therapist must be aware of both their potential for help and their potential for harm.

This work was supported, in part, by U.S.P.H.S. grants: MH-30906, MH-33422, and MH-37592.

DIFFERENTIAL DIAGNOSIS

The surest route to therapeutic simplicity is via differential diagnosis. Simply because a given psychopathological state is labeled anxiety does not ensure that it represents the same psychobiological process as another state labeled anxiety. Such resemblances may be due to overlapping final common pathways derived from distinct pathogeneses or even to fortuitous resemblances.

The clinician is faced with the necessity of a detailed diagnostic exploration prior to prescription. *The Diagnostic and Statistical Manual of Mental Disorders III* (1980) of the American Psychiatric Association is an enormous help and should be familiar to all practitioners.

SYNDROMES WITH ANXIETY SYMPTOMS

The following syndromes, often considered anxious, must be diagnostically dissected before rational pharmacotherapy can be prescribed.

1. Adjustment Disorder with anxious mood
2. Generalized anxiety disorder
3. Simple Phobia
4. Phobia secondary to spontaneous panic attacks
5. Obsessive-compulsive disorder
6. Depersonalization disorder
7. Hypochondriasis
8. Social Phobia
9. Depression

Adjustment Disorder With Anxious Mood

Reactive anxiety appears to be simply a quantitative variant of normal apprehension. We shall only briefly review the numerous traits usually considered associated with simple apprehensive states; motor tension, autonomic hyperactivity, anxious expectation, vigilance, and scanning are common features. It is the typical anxious symptomatology of the person facing a severe danger associated with marked uncertainty, such as being drafted, getting divorced, taking a new job, etc. The precipitant is evident. The anxiety of many patients with sexual difficulties is often assumed to fall in this category, but this may, on occasion, be erroneous.

At times, sexual difficulties are explained on the basis of a vicious cycle reaction due to some temporary fluctuation, so that erectile failure or premature ejaculation occurs. This is reacted to with anxiety and preoccupation concerning the possibility of failure, which in turn impairs sexual performance.

The psychotherapeutic approach emphasized by Masters & Johnson (1970), which takes the experience of sexual pleasure out of the performance arena by forbidding intercourse, is clearly calculated to break up this vicious cycle. Also, it is not clear that anxiety as a distressing affect is in itself sufficient to impair sexuality. However, it is clear that anxiety interferes with the sensual focus by intrusive apprehensive imagery.

Treatment of adjustment disorder with anxious mood

Work by Rickels (1966) has indicated that short duration, acute, anxious states of a reactive nature respond as well to placebo as to medication. There are anecdotal reports concerning the utility of benzodiazepines in facing specific dangers such as in bullfighting and going to the dentist.

Simple reactive anxiety needs little more than support. The use of medication is questionable, except perhaps small doses of an antianxiety agent, primarily for placebo value. Certainly, antipsychotic or antidepressant agents seem unwarranted.

Generalized Anxiety Disorder

Such patients seem simply to have a chronic free-floating anxiety without either panic attacks or phobic avoidance. Many such patients may actually have panic attacks which go unrecognized and have not led to phobic behavior. Since panic attacks are periodic phenomena, some patients have a self-limited series of panic attacks, develop expectant anxiety, have the panic attacks cease in the natural course of the illness, and are left with a chronic tensional state.

Treatment of generalized anxiety disorder

If panics are actually present, appropriate medication (antidepressants, Xanax), may be very helpful. Otherwise, benzodiazepines are appropriate.

Simple Phobia

A large number of patients feel relatively normal except directly on exposure to a specific phobic object or situation, e.g., elevators, cats, public speaking, etc., but do not have spontaneous panic attacks.

The clearest group of phobics seem to have an ingrained stimulus response association so that perceiving certain stimuli immediately fires off panicky sensations, leading, in turn, to marked anticipatory anxiety with regard to the proximal causal situation and consequent avoidance behavior. The cat phobic will not only become panicky instantly upon seeing a cat in the same room, but will apprehensively call ahead to friends before visiting them to make sure that they don't have a cat. Therefore, the entire simple phobic reaction consists of three components: the acute immediate situational reaction, the secondary anticipatory anxiety, and the tertiary avoidant behavior. The avoidant behavior is salient and results in this specific phobia level.

The degree of secondary anticipatory anxiety relates to the confidence of the patient that he can avoid the situational panic. Patients who are phobic of unusual objects, e.g., snakes, are usually as relaxed as anyone. Patients who are phobic of objects that may surprisingly appear, e.g., pigeons, may be chronically anxious, unless they are in a safe, enclosed area. Then they may become anxious about having to leave safety. The extreme case is the high level of chronic anticipatory anxiety suffered by patients with unavoidable spontaneous panic attacks, as described below.

Treatment of simple phobia

It is not clear if the situation-bound phobias will respond to antianxiety agents, such as the benzodiazepines. It seems reasonable that treatment with benzodiazepines might allow an expansion of behavior into the avoided areas, resulting in a decrease in apprehension, leading to *in vivo* extinction. There have been reports of the use of intravenous diazepam in such a context. However, evidence that exposure therapy is regularly successful in such patients is clear. Benzodiazepines should be reserved for treatment-refractory patients.

Phobia Secondary to Spontaneous Panic Attacks

The panic state is characterized by a sudden crescendo of terror accompanied by cardiorespiratory distress, dizziness, and paresthesias, and occasionally depersonalization. At times, the feeling of terror is paramount and the autonomic symptomatology is not discerned.

The outstanding characteristic of this syndrome is that spontaneous panic attacks usually precede the development of the massive free-floating tension-anxiety. The chronic anxiety represents the helpless anticipation of the irregularly recurrent panic attacks. The panic attack is the proximal inciting cause of the chronic anxiety state, which then leads to the variety of phobic avoidances used by the patient, who hopes to prevent a recurrence of the panics or at least guarantee easy, quick access to help and safety if he becomes panicked.

Phobic avoidance is usually related to being alone, or being blocked from aid, or travelling alone; it may misleadingly be referred to as agoraphobia. However, phobic patients with spontaneous panic attacks may have many different situational avoidances, but similar medication-response patterns.

One diagnostic headache is that patients will often deny spontaneous panics since they have figured out some reason for them. Therefore, they don't consider them as coming out of the blue but as due to some specific interpersonal or intrafamilial problem. One must persist with the patient in asking him to list all recent panic attacks. On being pressed for examples, they often will describe situations in which the panic attack was completely startling, with no apparent stimulus.

Some patients suffer from situationally predisposed panic attacks that are not entirely spontaneous, in the sense of being utterly surprising. For instance, certain patients instantly become panicky on attempting to drive. The response is immediate and unequivocal. Such patients have a condition entirely similar to the phobias that are immediately reactive to specific objects or situations, and no surprise occurs after the very first panic.

However, other patients with so-called driving phobias will irregularly become panicky while driving. They often link the panic to situations that make the driving somewhat more nerve-racking such as prolonged driving of long distances away from home or on the parkway. Nonetheless, the reaction is not immediate or regular. However, it is possible that these patients will not have panic attacks under any other circumstances. In this sense, their panics are not entirely spontaneous or surprising but are situationally limited and predisposed. Nonetheless, their medication-response patterns are like the phobias associated with apparently spontaneous panic attacks.

Yet another variant is a patient who has apparent episodic autonomic discharges that are not clearly panics. In particular, sudden feelings of dizziness or unsteadiness may occur with development of secondary anticipatory anxiety and avoidance behavior. Those patients who have developed separation anxious patterns in childhood often present gastrointestinal rather than cardiorespiratory symptomatology, i.e., diarrhea and cramps.

Finally, some patients only have panic attacks but do not develop avoidant behavior. Such people do not have a phobic disorder but rather a panic disorder.

Patients with panic disorder frequently develop hypochondriacal concerns about cardiac functioning. Therefore, they may develop apprehensive feelings about sexual exertion. They also may come to believe, usually incorrectly, that the excitement of sexual intercourse may actually precipitate a panic attack. This fosters sexual avoidance.

Treatment of panic disorders

Spontaneous or situationally predisposed panics can be blocked through the use of both tricyclic antidepressants and MAO inhibitors. Although the panics respond within a few weeks, or even earlier, the chronic tensional expectant anxiety requires a subsequent period of extinction, prior to the cessation of avoidance maneuvers.

Interestingly, the benzodiazepines, the meprobamate-like drugs, alcohol and barbiturates are all useful in decreasing the chronic anticipatory anxiety but are of no value in the panic attacks. The antidepressant stops spontaneous panic attacks, but is of no value for the chronic anxiety. This clearly indicates that these are two markedly different processes; the panic attacks are not simply the quantitative extension of chronic anxiety. Further, panic anxiety, so defined, is refractory to antipsychotics and may be exacerbated by them.

Because alcohol and barbiturates decrease their chronic anxiety, such patients frequently become addicted as they continually raise the self-administered dosage in the hope that their panics will also be relieved.

Recently, an atypical benzodiazepine, alprazolam, has been shown to be an effective treatment for panic disorders. There are also reports that alprazolam is an effective antidepressant. Some concern has been expressed about the need for slow withdrawal of this medication to prevent rebound anxiety. Alprazolam is clearly a useful agent, especially in those who cannot or will not tolerate tricyclics and MAOIs.

Obsessive-Compulsive Disorder

The obsessive-compulsive neurotic does not primarily complain about anxiety but rather about obsessions and compulsions. Anxiety only becomes manifest if rituals are interfered with.

Occasionally, the patient has an unrecognized depressive component which has exacerbated his obsessive-compulsive symptomatology and presents as a ruminative tension state. These patients are usually agitated depressives and will respond to the treatment of agitated depression by a return to their obsessional baseline.

Since the obsessive-compulsive patient is often preoccupied with stern morality and concerns about contamination, the sexual area is frequently highly charged and conflicted.

Treatment of obsessive-compulsive disorder

The psychopharmacologic approach to obsessive-compulsive neurosis has been disappointing. Practically every agent has been claimed to be effective in this condition. The reason for this peculiar state of affairs is that the obsessive-compulsive neurosis is often markedly exacerbated by a supervening agitated depression. Patients may increase hand-washing from 10 times a day to 100 times a day. The diagnostician may misperceive the salient handwashing compulsion as the central psychopathological issue rather than the affective disorder. Anything that will alleviate the affective disorder, e.g., phenothiazines or tricyclic agents, will reduce the sharply exacerbated compulsive symptomatology. However, the patient returns to his baseline state.

Recently, there have been persuasive reports that chlormipramine has specific value in obsessive-compulsive states over and above its antidepressant effect. Unfortunately, this medication is not yet available in the United States.

Depersonalization Disorder

This is a difficult syndrome to treat in which the primary experience seems to be that of depersonalization and/or derealization. Secondary to this there is reactive anxiety. However, it is possible that the depersonalization may be secondary to the anxiety since depersonalization is frequently reported as a concomitant of the panic attack in the so-called phobic anxiety depersonalization syndrome.

Depersonalization can be a complication of obsessive-compulsive neurosis or depression. For some reason, in American psychiatry severe depersonalization is regularly thought to be associated with schizophrenia. However, there seems to be no more reason to link depersonalization to schizophrenia than to any of the other severe disorders accompanied by marked affective disturbance.

Treatment of depersonalization disorder

If the patient is not having panic attacks, the depersonalization and secondary anxiety are quite refractory to any of our usual treatments. Sargant (1948) suggests intravenous methamphetamine.

Hypochondriasis

These are patients without manifest depression who are anxious and overconcerned with the possibility of being ill, requiring much reassurance. This is often referred to as somatizing.

The differential diagnosis of hypochondriacal neurosis is very involved. Somatic complaints are also a prominent feature of Bricquet's syndrome (polysystemic symptomatic complaint disorder), conversion reactions, depression, and panic disorders.

A careful differential diagnosis is indicated since quite specific pharmacotherapy is available for the nonhysterical disorders, whereas pharmacotherapy for hysterical disorders regularly results in exacerbation of the syndrome and intolerable side effects.

Treatment of hypochondriasis

In general, hypochondriasis is difficult to treat. The patients react sharply and negatively to side effects, frequently refusing to increase the dosage or covertly discarding the medication.

Apparently sedative agents are well accepted by this group so that diazepam may be more beneficial than chlordiazepoxide.

Depression

A very important differential diagnosis must be made between anxiety and agitation. Agitated patients are regularly tense and anxious. However, tense-anxious patients are not regularly agitated. The differential diagnosis revolves about the fact that the agitated depressive almost always has a massive pervasive inability to experience pleasure and has no interest in usually rewarding areas. This may occur without experiencing sadness or mood change; nonetheless, this defines agitation as an aspect of depression. Since such patients are often misleadingly called anxious depressives, a distinction must be made between anxiety and agitation.

The agitated patient will manifest both anxious symptomatology and marked motor facilitation. He paces, wrings his hands, and pleads in a loud vociferous fashion. One possibility is that depressive patients suffer from an inhibition of their pleasure evaluative center.

While the anxious patient responds to the anticipation of pain, the agitated patient acts as if in actual pain and complains of severe psychic distress. It is well known that the pain experience is a combination of the afferent pain sensation and the central evaluative reaction (often called distress). The agitated person acts as if his threshold for pain evaluation had been lowered. Some behavior, i.e., hand-wringing, cuticle picking, head banging, seem understandable as counter-irritative maneuvers resembling mustard plasters in their masking effect.

We now recognize that there are many different depressive states. We distinguish between depressive states where the mood disturbance is autonomous, that is, unresponsive to life changes and depressive states that are mood reactive. This latter group may partially cheer up when good things happen, but then slumps. Associated with the autonomous depressions are vegetative symptoms such as insomnia, loss of appetite, markedly decreased interest in sexual activity, and inability to gain pleasure from sexual activity. Depressed males often develop erectile incapacity.

Mood reactive depressions, however, are frequently associated with oversleeping, overeating, high degrees of interpersonal sensitivity to rejection, and a generally apathetic attitude. Surprisingly, these patients often retain the ability to respond positively to direct sexual engagement, although they frequently will not pursue such possibilities. Their sensitivity to interpersonal rejection, however, often makes their romantic relationships fraught with anxiety and disappointment. Having been burned repeatedly, such patients may withdraw from the possibilities of sexual relationships and, in general, conduct a socially avoidant lifestyle.

Treatment of depression

There is extensive literature on the treatment of depression. For many patients, medication is essential for their improvement. Recent efforts indicate that typical autonomous depressions respond well to tricyclic antidepressants, whereas, mood reactive depressions respond preferentially to MAO inhibitors.

Social Phobia

Social phobics are dominated by fear of humiliation or embarrassment. Therefore, they avoid situations in which they may fail while under the scrutiny of others. They develop marked anticipatory anxiety and avoid such situations.

Although social phobics are usually considered with regard to public performances such as public speaking or behavior at social events such as a party, it should be obvious that social phobia is particularly relevant to the intimacies of sexual relationships.

Male failures in sexual performance lead to poignant distress, partial erection, and premature ejaculation, which regularly lead to a vicious cycle terminating both in failure and avoidance.

Female inability to achieve excitement and orgasm is frequently dissimulated to avoid humiliation, thus preventing adequate therapeutic engagement (see Chapter 3).

Treatment of social phobia

Until recently, social phobia was considered to be entirely the outcome of intrapsychic conflict or unfortunate learning experiences. Therefore, the treatment emphasis was on dynamic or behavioral psychotherapy.

Although the cause of this illness is still poorly understood, recent studies have indicated that medication may play an important role in the treatment of social phobia. Preliminary work at the New York State Psychiatric Institute Anxiety Clinic, under the leadership of Michael Liebowitz, M.D. and Abby Fyer, M.D., have shown that both beta blockers and monoamine oxidase inhibitors can be surprisingly useful in the alleviation of social phobia. These treatments cannot be stated to have been established and, in fact, necessary procedural control studies are just getting underway. Nonetheless, the clinician may consider these agents if faced with an intractable situation. Benzodiazapines, on the other hand, although extensively used, do not seem particularly successful.

SEXUAL SIDE EFFECTS OF PSYCHOTROPIC MEDICATION

The unfortunate fact is that all classes of psychotropic medication may impair sexuality at the levels of desire, arousal, and orgasm at some dosage and in some patients, while others are not affected. These effects are often either missed or misunderstood. This is particularly true because often at the beginning of medication treatment patients may have substantial alleviation of their distressing affective states and actually improve in sexual pleasure and performance. Depressed patients, who may have completely lost interest in, and the capacity for, sexual activity, may have their mood normalization accompanied by a marked increase in sexual activity. Therefore, subsequent sexual difficulties are unlikely to be attributed to the antidepressant medication.

Interference with the Orgasm Reflex

It has only recently become recognized that the monoamine oxidase inhibitors may prevent orgasm in some patients and this effect seems to be dose related. This is particularly unexpected because this may occur even though a person's capacity for desire and arousal are often not impaired. Therefore, males may have converted into a pharmacological phenocopy of the spontaneously occurring pathological state of ejaculatio retardata. Women who regularly achieve orgasm may suddenly find themselves unable to do so. Since the possibility of this side effect is seldom discussed, they regularly attribute their anorgastic state to some intrapsychic or interpersonal difficulty. This is further complicated by the fact that this side effect may wax and wane and it is not unusual that after a period of orgastic disability the reflex may return to normal.

The pathophysiological basis for this disturbance is unknown. It is often considered to be due to anticholinergic side effects and, therefore, agents such as bethanacol are prescribed. There are numerous anectodal reports that this agent may be helpful in restoring the orgasm reflex; however, controlled data are still missing. Since bethanacol is safe and well tolerated, a trial of 50–100 mgs daily in an attempt to deal with this difficulty seems worthwhile.

Tricyclic antidepressants, which are substantially more anticholinergic than the monoamine oxidase inhibitors, are more often accompanied by difficulty in the excitement-engorgement phase, leading to erectile and engorgement difficulties rather than anorgasmia. The tricycylic antidepressants are also often reported to produce a state of relative sexual anesthesia in which genital stimulation is experienced as dulled and unpleasurable. In my experience, this is particularly likely the more anticholinergic the agent and at higher doses. For instance, amitriptyline (Elavil) is frequently associated with this side effect. When the patient is switched to desmethylimipramine (Norpramin), this side effect will often sharply decrease. I have seen some patients who, after an initial improvement from such a medication switch, experience a slow return of their sexual hypesthesia.

It is of some interest that trazodone (Desyrel), a relatively new antidepressant that is conspicuous for lack of anticholinergic side effects, has been reported associated with the rare occurrence of priapism. This can be a sexual catastrophe insofar as an unrelieved episode of priapism may result in structural impairment of erectile ability.

Among the worst medication offenders are the beta blockers which frequently interfere with the excitement/engorgement phase and may also block sexual desire. These agents may also result in depression and diminish feelings of pleasure.

In general, all of the sympatholytic agents used in the treatment of hypertension are suspect for sexual toxicity. The diuretics, however, are substantially less problematic, but can also cause impotence in some patients.

Inhibition of sexual desire may occur with any of the above agents. The benzodiazapines or minor tranquilizers are substantially free of sexual side effects. However, their prolonged use of high doses may incur a loss of sexual desire in a small number of cases.

For patients with spontaneous panic attacks who have their sexual functioning impaired by tricycylic antidepressants or monoamine oxidase inhibitors, alprazolam (Xanax), may prove a very valuable substitute. To date, there is no evidence that alprazolam impairs sexual functioning.

Another potentially valuable agent that is not available as yet, at least in the United States, is the specific MAO B inhibitor Deprenyl. This drug may have the same benefits as currently available MAO inhibitors with substantially fewer side effects.

Dosing Strategy

Only one drug at a time should be initiated, since the incidence of side effects increases rapidly with multiple drug administration. If several drugs are started simultaneously it is impossible to correctly attribute side effects to the offending drug.

It must be acknowledged that even in apparently clear-cut cases the best use of psychotropic agents is frequently found by trial and error. Therefore, it should be emphasized to the patient that he may need a change of medication after an adequate trial. The length of the adequate trial should be specifically stated so that there is no doubt as to how long ineffective medication will continue. One must emphasize that the patient is being shortchanged and possibly deprived of an effective drug if a drug which requires 4-6 weeks to work is tried for only one week. One may remind the patient of the length of his illness and point out the comparative insignificance of several more weeks of distress. (See Table 4.)

The frequency with which medication should be taken is debatable. Obviously, less frequent administration of medication results in greater convenience for the patient and lower risk of deviation from the prescribed routine. Furthermore, patients are often embarrassed by taking pills during the day.

Imipramine-like medications can often be given on a single daily dose schedule, about one hour prior to sleeping. There is a positive advantage to the single daily dose schedule for imipramine-like agents in that these agents appear to have a sedative peak, approximately 2 hours after drug administration, that has little to do with the long-lasting beneficial effects of the medication. A divided dosage schedule gives several obtunding sedative peaks during waking hours.

In spite of its many advantages, patients often balk at a single-dose

TABLE 4

Syndromes with Anxiety Aspects	Treatment
1. Reactive anxiety	No drug usually needed Anxiolytics may be prescribed
2. Generalized Anxiety Disorder	Antianxiety agents, e.g., benzodiazepine
3. Simple Phobia	Exposure Therapy
4. Phobia secondary to spontaneous panic attacks	Tricyclic antidepressants: MAO inhibitors, alprazolam
5. Obsessive Compulsive Disorder	Minor benefit from antianxiety agents; some patients are agitated depressives and should be treated as such Chlormipramine
6. Depersonalization	Refractory to usual treatments I.V. Methamphetamine?
7. Hypochondriasis	Diazepam?
8. Social Phobia	Experimental—MAOIs, Beta Blockers
9. Depression	TCAs, MAOIs, as indicated

schedule. They may not believe that the medication will be effective throughout a 24-hour period, or they may be frightened at the idea of taking many pills at once. Discussion and reassurance are necessary. Dosage schedules require individualization. The single daily dose schedule offers marked advantages. Medication with extended dosage release forms does not offer any advantage over simple tablets.

All relatively short-acting drugs should be given on a divided daily schedule. Recent evidence indicates that diazepam may be effective as single h.s. doses.

One should restrict to a sublethal dose the amount of drugs prescribed to a potential suicidal patient. This is particularly crucial with barbiturates, since even less than a 2-week supply may be fatal if consumed all at once. The doctor may be held legally responsible for such an oversight. I have stopped prescribing barbiturates in view of the availability of the safer benzodiazepines.

Establishing Effective Dosage

Effective doses of medication must be employed if one is to feel confident that the patient is receiving every chance of benefiting from the drug. For some reason, a considerable distinction is made by many doctors and drug houses between the levels of dosage suitable for outpatients and inpatients. The issue should be the safety of the patient and not the absolute magnitude of the dosage used. There is tremendous variation in the range of drug tolerance. This biological variability should impress the physician with the need for experimentation with the individual patient. Rough rules of thumb are available for determining ceilings that are rarely profitable to exceed. However, most pharmacotherapy suffers from being too conservative rather than too radical. If a medication appears to be only partially effective and the effects are not too disturbing or functionally impairing, it makes good sense to slowly increase the medication to the point at which the side effects become unacceptable, and then to drop back, thus maintaining maximum effect with minimum toxicity.

One must be particularly cautious about the method of initiating treatment with patients who have panic disorders. Approximately 20 percent of such patients have unusual sensitivity to imipramine, reacting as if it were a strong stimulant. They feel full of energy, jumping out of their skin and unable to sleep. The feeling is quite unpleasant and if not warned the patient may well believe that medication is too toxic to take.

My practice is to warn patients that this may occur and that it does not indicate that it is the wrong drug, but rather that it is the right drug. Imipramine is prescribed initially 25 mg h.s. and the patients are told to call me the next day in the morning. If the patients say they have slept reasonably well, then the dosage is increased in the same fashion as with depressive patients.

If the patients state that they have been unable to sleep all night, they are reassured and told to drop back to 10 mg per day taken in the A.M. The vast majority of such patients will tolerate this dosage. Surprisingly, this dosage may be entirely effective in blocking the panic attacks. The patients are then slowly raised as tolerance allows. A very occasional patient may require as little as 3 to 5 mg of imipramine a day. Evidently, imipramine is working in some fashion that is quite dissimilar from its usual antidepressant effect in these patients. However, most patients require the usual antidepressant dose of 200–300 mg/day.

It should be clear that our approach is that of tailoring the drug dosage schedule to the patient's biological peculiarities. Therefore, the patient should receive the maximum tolerable dose. Exceeding a maximum adult dose of about 300 mg a day calls for EKG monitoring.

Monoamine oxidase (MAO) inhibitors, often produce a greater therapeutic effect when increased from the usual range. Slow drug increments, closely monitored with attention to the appearance of side effects such as orthostatic hypotension, are often feasible and rewarding.

Close observation and treatment by a clinician skilled in the use of drugs should be the basis of good medication practices. Of course, if a doctor plans to employ an unusual dosage schedule, the risks should be explained to the patient in advance. It might be advantageous for the doctor to obtain a signed consent from the patient indicating his knowledge that the doctor is utilizing a therapy course differing from common practice. It must be pointed out that often the patients who require unusual methods are those least capable of reasonably judging these issues and they are likely to react in an anxious, irrational fashion. Therefore, the clinician's act of self-protective caution may be damaging for such patients.

The adjustment of dosage demands careful attention. It should be recognized that the effective major psychotropic agents act over long periods of time. Therefore, minor shifts in timing and dosage are rarely of any consequence. Having set as an initial goal determination of the greatest tolerable dose, one should not deviate from this course prior to the achievement of the maximum clinical improvement considered likely. The attempt to titrate symptomatology by continually altering the dosage from interview to interview is an expression of the therapist's anxiety and overcompliance rather than rational procedure. A patient's clinical condition fluctuates, and it is the long-term trend rather than the short-term perturbation with which we are ultimately concerned. Patients will often pressure for minor changes, but it is usually not wise to make these adjustments simply to placate the patient; one must believe that the changes are otherwise warranted. Placation carries the message that the patient knows more than the doctor. Of course, if the patient's suggestion is valid, one should not hesitate to accept it and acknowledge the patient's good sense.

An even greater danger than therapeutic tinkering is therapeutic rigidity and inertia. Continued complaints of social or personal ineffectiveness may indicate either that treatment has not as yet proved effective but should be maintained as promising or that some innovation is required. Far too often patients are called upon to "work it through" without evidence that they do anything but suffer. We believe that six weeks without discernible progress usually indicates a need for review of treatment and possible innovation.

MAINTENANCE THERAPY AND LONG-TERM MANAGEMENT

My general strategy is to attempt to keep the patient in relatively good remission for at least six months prior to weaning off medication, except for the self-limited reactive anxiety.

The pharmacological treatment of phobias is often incomplete and should be augmented by directive-supportive psychotherapy, including desensitization, relaxation, and *in vivo* exposure techniques. Following dissolution of avoidant behavior, anxiolytic medication may be terminated in simple phobics.

However, patients with panic disorders have a periodic relapsing condition. A large percentage of such patients will relapse swiftly if they are panic-free for only approximately one month prior to drug termination, whereas a much smaller percentage will relapse after six months of treatment. However, even the group that does not immediately relapse will often relapse several years later and require treatment. However, this is easily accomplished so that it does not seem warranted to prescribe indefinite maintenance therapy.

I have little experience with long-term treatment of generalized anxiety disorder. It is my impression that such patients often promptly relapse on discontinuation of antianxiety agents and require indefinite treatment. Obsessive-compulsive, depersonalization, and hypochondriacal disorders appear to require chronic medication for moderate benefits.

CONCLUSION

Careful differential diagnosis of anxious and depressive states in patients with sexual disorders is a necessity. Appropriate diagnosis and prescription of medication is of great use for many patients and can serve as a very useful adjunct to appropriate psychotherapy.

Unfortunately, even medication that has proven its utility in relieving psychiatric symptoms may incur sexual difficulty in some cases. Therefore, the therapist must maintain a high degree of vigilance and balanced judgement concerning the advantages and deficits of these agents. (See also Chapter 5.)

CHAPTER 5

Treatment: An Integrated Approach

Psychodynamically oriented sex therapy combines behavioral interventions in the form of prescribed sexual interactions that are carried out by the couple at home, with psychodynamically oriented psychotherapy office sessions which are generally conducted conjointly (Kaplan, 1974).* The new antipanic medication has added a third dimension to this integrated approach, which has extended the benefits of sex therapy to patients with associated panic disorders.

Behavioral, dynamic and pharmacological methods play different roles in this treatment approach. Each has specific capabilities as well as specific limitations, but fortunately the shortcomings of one lie in the area of strength of the others, and together the three modalities constitute a comprehensive and effective treatment system.

Sexual therapy is considered the treatment of choice for the psychosexual dysfunctions which impair the genital phases of the sexual response cycle. This method is also ideally suited for treating sexual aversion disorders and the phobic avoidance of sex.

The objective of the behavioral aspect of treatment is to extinguish the patient's irrational sexual fears and to modify his avoidance of sex with systematic exposure to the previously avoided sexual situation. Some sexually phobic and aversive individuals are free of major psychopathology, enjoy good marriages, and are endowed with a normal biological capacity for panic. These patients may respond to *in vivo*

---

* Readers who are not familiar with psychodynamically oriented sexual therapy are referred to earlier works which describe the "New Sex Therapy" and its theoretical foundations (Kaplan, 1974, 1979, 1983).

desensitization, conducted in a supportive ambiance, without the need for any additional psychodynamic interventions. But the majority of couples with sexual aversion suffer from significant underlying neurotic conflicts, sexual guilts, and marital problems. More often than not they resist the behavioral modification of their sexual symptoms. When this occurs, brief dynamic techniques are used to deal with their deeper conflicts.

This combined approach is more effective and more rapid for treating sexual symptoms than psychoanalytic therapies by themselves. One reason is that the patient's current dismal sexual experiences reinforce his sexual avoidance which then acquires a "life of its own" and is maintained long after the original traumata which gave birth to his sexual fears have vanished. Therefore, sexual aversions often persist even after patients have worked long and hard to attain valid insights into their sexual conflicts and to improve their relationships, unless the dynamic aspect of therapy is supplemented by direct modification of the patient's habitual pattern of sexual avoidance (Kaplan, 1974, 1979).

Another advantage of this eclectic approach is that the behavioral interventions can facilitate the resolution of unconscious conflicts when the therapeutic process is conceptualized psychodynamically. The desensitization methods that are used for sexual phobias and aversion disorders tend to strip away the patient's psychological defenses and this can expose his deepest jealousies, insecurities and vulnerabilities. The flood of significant dreams, memories and associations, which this process frequently evokes, become the subject of dynamically oriented therapeutic exploration during the office sessions (Kaplan, 1974, 1979).

Antipanic medication can potentiate both the psychodynamic and the behavioral aspects of therapy in patients with sexual panic states. According to the principles of conditioning, exposure to a phobic object while the individual is in a state of relaxation will extinguish the phobic response (p. 38). Theoretically, it is irrelevant for the success of this procedure whether the required degree of tranquility is chemically induced or achieved by psychological means as long as the individual is mentally alert enough to perceive and make the connection between the phobic object and his calm inner state. Therefore, any substance which reduces anxiety without obtunding conscious awareness should facilitate fear extinction (Kaplan, 1956).

A number of behavior therapists have used alcohol (Kaplan, 1956), and short-acting barbiturates to aid systematic desensitization with this rationale (Brady, 1962).

However, the dose levels at which sedative substances diminish the fear response, also begin to impair perceptual processes and cloud conscious awareness. This narrow "therapeutic window" makes these agents less than perfect for *in vivo* desensitization.

The antipanic drugs, on the other hand, are ideally suited for facilitating fear extinction because their tranquilizing action is almost completely dissociated from any disturbance of the higher cortical functions or sensory awareness even at higher doses.

The efficacy of antipanic medications for treating agoraphobia in patients with panic disorders and also school avoidance in children with separation anxiety can be conceptualized along similar lines. It was on this theory that we first used antipanic drugs in conjunction with sex therapy for patients with sexual panic states, fully anticipating that these drugs would add to the effectiveness of the behavioral modification of the phobic avoidance of sex.

However, we had not expected to find that in a number of our couples with sexual panic states the concomitant use of these drugs with sexual therapy also seemed to enhance the dynamic and marital aspects of treatment.

MEDICATION AND SEX THERAPY

The disruptive panic attacks and intense separation anxieties that are experienced during the process of sex therapy by patients with sexual panic states interfere with the desensitization procedure and also with meaningful dynamic exploration of their underlying emotional conflicts. The protection from panic attacks and the relief from the hypersensitivity to rejection from the partner, which the antipanic drugs provide for patients with underlying panic disorders, enables us to treat some who would otherwise be entirely untreatable and makes the process of sex therapy more rapid and less stressful for others.

TCAs (tricyclic antidepressants) are considered the drugs of choice for panic disorder (see also Chapter 4). These were the first substances found to block panics without disturbing perception or clouding conscious awareness and they have been extensively investigated. The most widely used TCAs are: imipramine (Tofranil); desimipramine (Norpramine), its more rapidly acting derivative; amitryptyline (Elavil); and nortryptyline (Aventil) which is that drug's more rapidly acting metabolite (see Chapter 4). For patients with sexual panic states who do not respond to TCAs, or cannot tolerate their side effects, MAOIs (monoamine oxidase inhibitors) are effective second-line drugs which also block panics. As an alternative or, if the side effects of MAOIs or TCAs present difficulties for the patient, alprazolam (Xanax), which has fewer sexual side effects than the TCAs and the MAOIs, is a good substitute for or addition to TCAs. We have used all of these medications in conjunction with sex therapy for patients with sexual panic states.

Most patients respond to the first-time drugs and experience few if any side effects. But in the light of Klein's finding that up to 85 percent of patients with panic disorder can be brought under good control with antipanic medication (Klein et al., 1980b), it is well worth the therapist's time and effort to patiently persist until the right medication is found and adjusted to an effective dose, even when a patient is difficult to medicate.

Clinical Management

In the usual course of treatment the patient's phobic avoidance of sex would be expected to diminish steadily with each therapeutically controlled exposure. Persistent negative reactions to assignments that are well conceived should always raise questions about medication. If the patient has not been medicated, then her psychiatric history should be reviewed to determine if a trial of medication makes sense. If the patient is already on medication, the dose may have to be raised or a second-line drug considered.

In the weekly review of her therapeutic experience, the patient is asked if she has experienced any panic attacks and what her general level of anxiety has been. A patient's report that she has not panicked could indicate that she is adequately medicated, but the absence of panics could also mean that she has managed to avoid the specific aspect of sex that triggers her phobic response. Therefore, if a patient with panic disorder is not making satisfactory progress, it might make sense to increase the dosage or to switch to another drug on a trial basis, even if she has reported no recent panic episodes.

Good drug responders typically report that they feel the familiar sensations which had in the past signaled an impending panic attack as they approached their sexual assignment, but to their surprise this does not materialize.

The sexual anxiety of good responders often diminishes with desensitization at the same rate as that of phobic patients with normal anxiety reactions. But some patients have only partial responses to medication, and their intense sexual anxiety persists even though they do not panic. Such individuals may simply require more frequent repetitions of the desensitization exercises than patients with simple sexual phobias.

Sexual Side Effects

TCAs and MAOIs can impair the desire, excitement, and orgasm phases of the male and female sexual response cycle (see Chapter 4).

Most of the sexual side effects that are seen with these drugs are dose-related and are more likely to occur at the high dose levels used for depression, while a relatively small number of patients have sexual difficulties with the lower doses which often suffice for treating sexual panic states. Fortunately, these drug-induced sexual difficulties can often be corrected by lowering the dose of the drug, or by substituting another antipanic agent in the same class, or by switching to another type of medication. Some side effects, notably those affecting orgasm and ejaculation, can be managed by adding anticholinergic drugs and/or serotonin antagonists.*

Beta adrenergic blockers, which are being used for anxiety disorders by some clinicians, are the worst offenders and we do not like to use these drugs for patients with sexual complaints.

Some patients with sexual panic disorders whose sexual responses have not been altered become obsessively concerned that their medication is making them impotent and want to discontinue the drug which is so helpful to them.

Other patients whose erectile dysfunction really is drug-related, or their spouses or therapists, are deeply convinced that the problem is psychogenic.

When the etiology of a patient's erectile disorder is not clear, we sometimes obtain objective evidence by monitoring his sleep erections with and without the suspected drug. We use a portable NPT monitor which the patient uses at home for two consecutive nights while taking his customary medication and we repeat the procedure after he has been drug-free for a sufficient period of time to clear the drug from his system. We then compare the two records with the patient and/or the couple within the therapeutic context of the office session.

This procedure was helpful in the following case:

Case Vignette #8: Walter

The patient was a 32-year-old single man who complained about impotence which he believed was being caused by Tofranil. Eight years previously, he had developed severe panic attacks with agoraphobia. Over the next 6 years he saw a number of therapists,

---

* Personal communication, D. Klein, 1986.

none of whom were able to help him. Finally, two years prior to his consultation with us, he saw a psychiatrist who prescribed Tofranil 250 mgm. The medication rapidly relieved the patient's symptoms, and his life changed. He entered the family business, began to socialize, and fell in love with a girl he wanted to marry. But he could not function sexually and she threatened to leave him.

The patient's impotence was clearly related to his performance anxiety, which was intensified by his sensitivity to rejection together with his partner's demands and threats. However, he resisted any suggestions of this nature and remained obsessed with the idea that Tofranil was causing the problem. He agreed to be tested with and without the drug and was startled to find that, if anything, he had a greater number of erections and these lasted longer when he was taking Tofranil. This confrontation with the psychogenic nature of his impotence was salutary in resolving his resistance to therapy.

In other cases, comparative NPT testing with and without medication provides objective evidence that a man's impotence is related to his medication, which saves patients from unnecessary surgery or inappropriate sex therapy.

Two-thirds of patients with panic states require medication only during treatment, while one-third can be expected to relapse unless they continue with drug therapy (Mavissakalian & Michelson, 1986). Our experience with the sexaphobic patients we have treated with sex therapy and medication is similar. Three to six months after termination of therapy, and after the couple has integrated their new sexual adequacy, medication can be discontinued and in most cases the symptom will not return.

Relief of the Sexual Symptom

Psychopharmacologists have used antipanic medication with great success to treat the symptoms of panic disorder, but the therapeutic power of these drugs is even greater when they are used within a holistic, psychodynamic context that considers the patient within his total environment, and not only for the relief of his target symptom.

As a simple example, it has often been noted that agoraphobic patients with panic disorders suddenly find themselves less vulnerable and frightened of rejection after they have been medicated. They then feel freer to express their anger. This new assertiveness is often constructive. However, problems can arise when individuals who have been repressing a great deal of rage at their husbands, wives, or employers are abruptly released from the constraints of their separation fears by medication. Marriages break up so frequently after patients have received TCAs that Tofranil has been dubbed the "divorce drug" by some psychopharmacologists.

The risks of precipitating self-destructive acting out is minimized when the therapist understands the patient and his significant relationships in depth and when he has good therapeutic rapport with him. He is then in a position to confront the patient with the harmful consequences of his impulsive behavior and to help him integrate his new emotional independence constructively into the fabric of his life.

In a similar vein, antipanic medication can relieve the patient's phobic response to sex, but the drugs have no direct effect on the anticipatory anxiety that has built up over the years, nor can they cure the emotional damage that was caused by the patient's long-standing sexual avoidance.

The relief of sexual panic with medication in adult life can be compared with the surgical correction of a 30-year-old woman's congenitally malformed leg. She will not be able to go out dancing as soon as her leg heals. She has grown up disabled. She has had to sit by while others were learning to dance and has worked out a system of adaptations and defenses that have become an integral part of her personality. She will need time, practice, and encouragement to learn to use and strengthen her newly corrected limb, and she will require a comprehensive program of therapy and rehabilitation before she will be able to fully enjoy dancing and before her self-image can change from crippled to whole.

Similarly, the elimination of a long-standing sexual symptom by means of medication does not insure that a couple's sexual relationship will automatically become wonderful. Other problems which could have been obscured by their sexual difficulties may surface. Or a husband may need help in dealing with the new demand on him to "perform" that was created by the cure of his wife's sexual avoidance.

When a pattern of sexual fear and aversion develops as early as adolescence, psychosexual development is interrupted at a critical point. A youngster's avoidance of sex at a time when his friends are beginning to fall in love and are developing sexual and heterosocial skills can have devastating psychological consequences.

It usually takes time and considerable additional psychotherapeutic work with both partners to help them adjust to the new system. Most helpful of all to complete their psychosexual rehabilitation is the reinforcement provided by repeated positive sexual experiences without the old panic.

Engaging the Couple in Sex Therapy

Avoidance is an absolute obstacle to the extinction of the phobic response and treatment will fail if the patient continues to avoid sex. But overcoming long-standing sexual fears is difficult, no matter how highly motivated a person is to improve his sexual inadequacy. The therapist's effectiveness in persuading couples to commit themselves to the stressful behavioral programs entailed in sex therapy is a critical factor in the success of treatment of sexual panic states.

It is our practice to provide patients and their spouses with accurate information about the nature of their sexual disorder and to explain the process of treatment to them. This helps engage those individuals who are primarily moved by reason and will make the effort to overcome their avoidance only if they clearly understand the logic of the procedure.

Others can be engaged in this difficult treatment process on the strength of their trust in the therapist and by their relationship with him or her. The power of the therapeutic alliance is often amplified by the intense positive transferences which patients who are in sex therapy frequently develop. The therapist uses this leverage to help the patient overcome his compelling urge to avoid the crucial therapeutic exposures.

Love for the partner, commitment to his happiness, compassion for his sexual needs, and a sense of fairness are the motivating forces for others.

The fear of abandonment is a powerful motive for patients who have associated panic disorders. Some of these individuals do not commit themselves wholeheartedly to the treatment program until they are faced with the risk they are taking of losing their spouse unless they are willing to make the effort to improve the sexual relationship.

Some patients cannot overcome their compelling urge to avoid the dreaded sexual situation because their symptom represents a defense against significant unconscious conflicts about sex. In such cases, the patient will have to gain insight into the underlying neurotic processes that are paralyzing him before he can be expected to relinquish his defensive avoidance.

Finally, patients with panic disorder may simply be too apprehensive about experiencing terrifying panic attacks in sexual situations to be able to risk exposure. These patients are right in sensing that they are too anxious to benefit from sex therapy and the therapist should not attempt to persuade them to undergo the behavioral exercises until they are adequately protected against their panics with medication.

The Couple as Cotherapists

I find it useful to think of panic disorders as analogous to diabetes. Both are biological abnormalities that have profound effects on a person's life and in both disorders the cornerstone of successful management is patient education and attitude.

The modern diabetologist teaches his patients the facts about their disease, their medication, and the rules of glucose metabolism. He trains them to monitor their own blood sugar readings and, most important, he must persuade them to take responsibility for their own health. Patients must learn to adjust their insulin to their food intake, exercise, and stress on a continuing basis in order to keep their blood sugar levels within a nonpathogenic range. They are more likely to succeed in this time-consuming and vexing task if they understand that this is necessary to prevent their becoming blind or impotent, and that no one else can do this for them.

I use a similar approach to enlist the couple's active participation in the management of their sexual panic disorder. The possibility of a good therapeutic result is greatly increased when the patient and her partner are well informed about the nature of sexual panic states, the potential benefits of medication, and the rules of desensitization, and if they adopt a responsible realistic, and constructive attitude towards their problem.

As with the diabetic patient who must learn to become aware of his blood sugar level by taking readings under different circumstances, patients with panic disorder must develop an acute awareness of their level of anxiety. A variety of techniques can be used to help patients who are not sufficiently "in touch" with their feelings learn how to "read" their emotional reactions to sexual experiences accurately.

Teaching patients to rate their level of tension on a scale of 0 to 10 focuses their attention on their previously unrecognized inner sensations. The emergence of difficult material during the office sessions creates the opportunity for raising a phobic patient's consciousness to her anxiety. When the therapist senses that his patient's level of tension is rising, he can stop the discussion and alert her to this:

Therapist: "I think you are becoming anxious now that we are talking about your husband's sexual frustration. If 'ten' is a panic attack, and 'zero' is perfect tranquility, how would you rate your anxiety at this moment?"

The ratings become part of the therapy "language," very much like the glycohemoglobin numbers become part of the diabetologist's dialogue with his patient.

> *Therapist:* "I want you to let him touch your breast, but if anxiety level rises above seven, back off and try it again the next evening."
> *Husband:* "She was great—she really did it—but I think she pushed herself too hard. I saw her really getting panicky. I think she was up to 'nine' or even 'ten.' "

The patient learns the rules of fear extinction and the destructive consequences of her avoidance of the sexual assignments. These conceptual tools help her assume responsibility for her own progress and to accept the necessity of enduring some discomfort in order to obtain her goals. The patient needs to understand that she cannot avoid all her anxieties without paying a very high price. This is essential if she is to commit herself to do the exercises for herself, rather than do this half heartedly for her husband or her therapist.

It is comforting for the patient to realize that she can control the extinction process and set her own pace without compromising her therapeutic objective. Patients relax when they learn that they need deal only with a small, manageable piece of their anxiety at any one time and that their anxiety will eventually abate if they simply persist and repeat the exercises often enough. It is also important for the wider goal of helping patients rid themselves of the guilt and shame they may feel about their "weakness" to get them to understand that it is "okay" to feel anxious and that it is counterproductive to allow themselves to get too panicky. When they feel their apprehension becoming too intense, backing off and trying again is not cowardly but constructive.

> *Therapist:* "I want you to look at his penis, but I don't want you to let your anxiety level go above 'six,' so if you start to feel too anxious, close your eyes, wait until you get down to 'one,' and try to look again. See if you can increase the time it takes you to reach 'six' to about two minutes this week."

The partner's full understanding of the patient's panic disorder and his unambivalent participation in and commitment to the desensitization process is extremely helpful and can make the difference between treatment success and failure.

EXTINCTION OF THE PHOBIC RESPONSE

It is the consensus of behaviorally oriented clinicians that a program of systematic, therapeutically controlled exposure to the phobically avoided situation is the most effective behavioral method for extinguishing phobic symptoms of all kinds (Marks, 1978, 1980). The behavioral aspects of sex therapy are based on this principle and rely mainly on *in vivo* desensitization to modify the phobic avoidance of sex. The essence of this technique is to expose the patient gradually and progressively to the feared and previously avoided sexual situation under calm and pleasurable circumstances.* In the course of this procedure, the phobic patient is instructed to remain physically and emotionally in the presence of a small and manageable piece of the feared sexual situation. For example, the patient with a phobic avoidance of sex might be encouraged to force himself to remain in the presence of a nude woman until his anxiety diminishes, although this initially makes him anxious and apprehensive. But he is also given the comforting limits that he is not to touch her, nor to attempt to have intercourse. In the usual case, the patient's anxiety will rapidly abate when he is relieved of performance pressure and he will typically begin to experience pleasure. Then he will be instructed to go on to the next step. The repeated pairing of the previously avoided sexual situation with new calm and pleasurable feelings progressively weakens the old unwanted sex = fear associations, while the simultaneous experience of sex and pleasure will then establish this new and desired connection.

The *in vivo* desensitization of patients with sexual aversions and panic disorders poses special problems because of the intense stress and anxiety that these individuals tend to experience when they are exposed to previously avoided sexual situations in the course of sex therapy. For example, the sensate focus exercises which are ordinarily therapeutic can be terrifying for patients with sexual panic states.

Sensate Focus

The Sensate Focus (SF) exercises were invented by Masters and Johnson when sex therapy was in its infancy and remains the best method devised to this date for the *in vivo* desensitization of simple sexual phobias (Masters & Johnson, 1970).

During the SF exercises, the partners take turns gently and leisurely caressing each other's nude body. During this assignment, the genitals are not stimulated directly and intercourse and orgasm are proscribed.

---

* *In vivo desensitization* should be distinguished from *systematic desensitization*, a technique developed by Joseph Wolpe, which uses imagery of, but not physical exposure to, the phobic situation (Wolpe, 1958). Systematic desensitization has been disappointing for treating sexual disorders.

The simplicity of SF is deceptive and obscures its powerful therapeutic impact on sexually dysfunctional couples.

The SF exercises were originally devised to diminish performance anxiety. This is a major cause of impotence and also plays a significant role in the pathogenesis of other sexual disorders, including sexual panic states. In many cases, there is simply no better way to diminish performance anxiety than to take the anxious person "off the hook" of the pressure to perform by prohibiting intercourse and by shifting the goal from sexual performance to the sharing of pleasure. Quite often, the anxious impotent patient spontaneously becomes erect when he begins to focus on his pleasurable sensations and when he stops obsessing about his performance. This experience has more therapeutic efficacy than a hundred interpretations.

In addition, the SF exercises help to improve the blocked communications about sexual feelings that are often a problem for sexually troubled couples.

The SF exercises provide an ideal structure for extinguishing sexual fears and aversions and are extremely useful for treating sexual panic disorders. SF creates a safe, comfortable and nondemanding sexual ambiance over which the patient has control. The couple's sexual interactions are structured so that the male partner "stays with" the anxiety-provoking, previously avoided sexual situation for as long as it takes him to become comfortable. By interfering with his tendency to flee from sexual situations, the SF exercises provide the patient with the opportunity to allow his irrational anxieties to abate. This exposes him, sometimes for the first time in his life, to nudity, touching, kissing, and just being with a sexual partner, protected from performance fears and from the humiliation of failure and partner rejection. Simply remaining long enough with an attractive partner while he is free from pressure frequently allows the patient's natural sexual feelings to begin to emerge spontaneously.

Sensate Focus I begins the gradual and systematic step-by-step process of non-erotic touching that hopefully leads to the complete extinction of sexual anxiety. With the exception of those relatively few couples who have serious marital problems or major psychopathology and are therefore not appropriate candidates for this type of treatment, the majority of sexually phobic patients without panic disorders respond rapidly to the SF exercises. After one to three repetitions, they are ready to proceed to genital stimulation.

When body caressing no longer evokes anxiety and has become pleasurable, the couple proceeds to SF II. This assignment repeats SF I with the addition of the direct stimulation of the genitals. During this phase of treatment, orgasm is still prohibited, but the partners take turns caressing each other's genitalia gently and teasingly. The aim of this exercise is simply for the lovers to get accustomed to experiencing pleasure together, while performance is still deemphasized. At this stage, the vigorous, rhythmic type of stimulation that leads to the "plateau phase" of arousal and to orgasm is still proscribed. The pleasurable sensations and feelings evoked by sexual stimulation are strong reinforcers hastening the extinction process by reciprocal inhibition. SF II also serves to extinguish patients' fears and avoidance of their own and their partner's genitalia. This also diminishes the discomfort that some of these patients feel about becoming aroused in the presence of the partner.

After the phobic patient has been desensitized to exchanging genital stimulation with his partner and begins to feel comfortable being aroused in her presence, the next step may entail the experience of sharing extravaginal orgasm. During this phase of the extinction process which we call SF-III, the couple may be asked to learn to become comfortable stimulating themselves to orgasm in the partner's presence. If the patient is exceptionally guilty or embarrassed about masturbation because of his strict antisexual upbringing, or if he has severe neurotic masturbatory inhibitions, this step can be bypassed and the couple can go directly to the next phase which entails stimulating each other to orgasm, manually and/or orally if the latter is acceptable to the couple.

The experience of extravaginal orgasm in the partner's presence heightens the couple's level of intimacy and enhances their communication. They might learn that instead of being repelled, as they had feared, a partner can be excited by observing their self-pleasuring and arousal. These experiences also serve to desensitize those patients who fear the loss of control during sexual abandonment and orgasm.

If the patient has avoided using his masturbatory erotic fantasies when he is with his partner, we might at this point suggest that he deliberately evoke these images while she is physically stimulating him. When a couple is able to share and accept each partner's most private thoughts and wishes, sexual shame and anxiety diminish even further, helping to create trust and to deepen the intimate bond between them.

When these precoital experiences no longer evoke anxiety and avoidance, intromission and nondemanding coital movements without orgasm are frequently assigned. Full intravaginal intercourse then completes the desensitization process.

This gradual, systematic exposure to increasingly intense erotic experiences mirrors and condenses into a brief time period the normal sequence of sexual development that young persons in our society usually experience. For sexually phobic patients who have missed this important learning and rehearsal phase, the sexual assignments, together with the therapist's support and encouragement, provide an important corrective experience.

Sensate Focus Exercises and Patients with Sexual Panic States

The sensate focus exercises, while excellent for treating simple sexual phobias and aversions, were not originally designed with panic disorder in mind. If used without consideration of the special vulnerability of these patients, they may evoke counterproductive panic reactions instead of reducing their sexual anxiety.

The experience of a certain amount of anxiety is an integral part of the desensitization process and is actually necessary for the success of this method because effective desensitization requires that exposure to the phobically avoided situation occur within an optimal range of anxiety.

If the patient feels no anxiety at all, desensitization is not taking place. Either he is not being exposed to the actual phobic trigger or the exposure is taking place at a level of intensity that is too low to be effective. But excessively high levels of anxiety are equally counterproductive and, in fact, may aggravate the patient's phobic avoidance (Kaplan, 1979). This conceptualization derives from learning theory (Chapter 3), according to which a patient's anxiety must diminish sufficiently while he is in the phobic situation in order that a new association between the previously feared sexual situation with an inner state of tranquility and comfort can be formed. Desensitization will not take place if the patient does *not* become tranquil when he is in the presence of the feared sexual object (Birch & Bitterman, 1949). Instead, if he panics, a negative conditioning process may occur which links sex with even more intense fear which can reinforce and strengthen the phobic response and make the patient worse.*

Patients with panic disorder tend to remain apprehensive about having a panic attack while they are doing the assignment. Their anxiety does not diminish in response to the usual psychological methods. Some of these patients can achieve the necessary state of tranquility only with medication.

Properly medicated patients do not experience panic attacks during

---

* The behavioral literature reports some success with "flooding" for the treatment of phobias. However, in our experience exposing the patient to the phobically avoided sexual situation while he is in a state of panic is not useful in the treatment of sexual panic states and may aggravate these conditions.

exposure. As they see that the feared panic attacks do not materialize, their sexual anxiety may diminish as rapidly as it does in phobic patients without panic disorders. However, some phobically anxious patients seem to have an incomplete response to medication. While they do not actually panic, their sexual anxiety diminishes exceedingly slowly during the exposure experiences.

Therapeutic Control of Anxiety

The therapeutic process should be conducted so that the patient's anxiety diminishes steadily and as rapidly as possible without rising to counterproductive heights. Maintaining a tight level of control over the therapeutic process is one of the most important and demanding functions of the dynamically oriented sex therapist (Kaplan, 1979).

In order to succeed in this critical task, the therapist must continually monitor the patient's response to each step of the treatment process. For this reason, we review the couple's experience with the sexual assignments in great detail at the beginning of each weekly office session. The therapist is in no position to devise the next assignment unless he has a clear mental image of how the couple reacted to last week's assignment. He needs to know how anxious the phobic partner became, whether she had a panic attack, and whether she avoided some threatening aspects of the assignment. The therapist must also find out if the patient had been able to stay in the phobic situation until her anxiety diminished because, again, this is *the* key issue in desensitization. It is useful to ascertain how sexual she felt because an increase in a patient's level of sexual arousal is an excellent indication that her anxiety is diminishing.

The partner's reactions are monitored in the same detail, and with the same persistence because his emotional and sexual status is highly material to the phobic patient's anxiety level and to the treatment outcome.

Individualizing the Pace and Intensity of Desensitization

The weekly analysis of the couple's sexual experience provides the therapist with the information he needs to fine tune the pace and intensity of the assignments to fit the patient's particular needs. This is also needed for adjusting the medication, all for the purpose of maintaining the patient's anxiety at a level optimally conducive to the extinction of his sexual phobia.

The majority of patients with psychosexual dysfunctions can be taken through the extinction process rapidly and become comfortable with the SF I and II exercises after two or three repetitions. Thus, Masters and Johnson, who rely heavily on this procedure, were able to cure over 80 percent of their patients with psychosexual dysfunctions in two weeks, with 14 daily sessions.

But patients who are intensely anxious require a much slower pace and the therapist should not give up if the panicky patient initially has negative responses to SF. Some highly anxious patients, especially those with phobic anxiety syndrome, need to proceed with very small increments and it may be necessary to repeat each step as many as 20 to 30 times to extinguish their intense phobic responses. But, if the SF exercises are individualized and modified, it is ultimately possible to get good results in many initially resistant cases.

Rosa's treatment (Case Vignette #1, p. 4) illustrates the difficulties of desensitizing patients with the more severe forms of phobic anxiety syndrome, which can occur even when they are medicated.

The SF exercises which her previous therapists had prescribed evoked intense anticipatory anxiety and Rosa had had several panic attacks in the course of her prior sex therapy. This aggravated her phobic avoidance of sex with her husband. Since her best efforts to comply with the therapist's assignments, no matter how difficult these were for her, only made her worse, she began to feel hopeless and became depressed.

In her treatment with us she was protected by medication and experienced no panic attacks. But she remained so intensely anxious that the SF exercises had to be deferred for several months of preparatory work and even thereafter, the desensitization steps had to be made much smaller than usual.*

But Rosa's sexual fears and avoidance slowly diminished, and eventually she had an excellent response to treatment.

Partial Sexual Phobias and Aversions

The Sensate Focus exercises are effective for desensitizing patients with generalized sexual phobias, but this method is not appropriate when aversive responses are limited to specific circumscribed aspects of sex. The desensitization schedules for such patients must be individualized to expose them to the correct phobic stimulus, otherwise treatment cannot succeed.

---

* For example, initially she was instructed merely to lie close to Richard on the bed watching TV while he wore his undershorts, and she a nightgown. This had to be repeated for two weeks before she became comfortable enough to go to the next step.

The following case vignettes illustrate two different behavioral programs. One is typically used for the extinction of penetration phobias, and the other was specifically devised for the desensitization of a patient's aversive response to breast stimulation.

Case Vignette #9: Bridget

The patient was a 26-year-old working class, Roman Catholic, Irish immigrant woman. She had been married for four years to Bryan, 30 years old, who was from a similar cultural background. The marriage had not been consummated because Bridget panicked whenever Brian attempted to have intercourse with her. The patient's panic reactions were triggered specifically by vaginal penetration. She had no anxiety about any other kind of sexual activity. In fact, she greatly enjoyed foreplay with Bryan and she was orgastic with clitoral stimulation.

The couple loved each other and were eager to have children. Both were very distressed by their inability to consummate the marriage.

This patient had a classic panic disorder. Her history revealed that she had suffered from night terrors and panic attacks as a child. She was so excessively attached to and inseparable from her mother that this became a family joke. Two aunts were described as "very nervous," while one uncle and two cousins were alcoholics. As a child she was terrified by thunderstorms, phobically avoided horses and doctors, and was very uncomfortable in social situations with adults.

Bridget was raised in a large, warm, happy family. Her parents loved each other and their children. Her mother, a loving, "no-nonsense" woman, taught Bridget to face her anxieties and to overcome her avoidances. These constructive attitudes served her well; apart from her avoidance of penetration and a few minor phobias, this young woman was not disabled by her panic disorder.

Cultural factors also played a role in this case. Bridget's mother was a devout Roman Catholic who imbued her eight children with deeply religious attitudes. Bridget, who was especially close to her mother, accompanied her to church every Sunday. The children attended parochial schools where the nuns taught her that sex was a sin unless within marriage and for the purpose of procreation. Bridget remembered that the children were instructed to put talcum powder on the surface of the water when bathing to avoid viewing their own nude bodies. She took these sexual prohibitions very much to heart.

It may be speculated that this patient's low panic threshold amplified and intensified the impact of her religious sexual training. This predisposed her to develop a phobic avoidance of intercourse, which did not go away on her wedding night.

Nothing would have been gained by using the SF exercises in this case, because the patient had no anxiety about and did not avoid body touching, genital stimulation, or sexual arousal with her husband. The behavioral aspects of this patient's treatment had to be specifically designed to gradually systematically accustom her to penetration.

The patient was not medicated because her religious beliefs prohibited contraception and she might have been impregnated during treatment.*

Treatment was difficult for Bridget. She was extremely apprehensive about penetration and the behavioral increments had to be made exceedingly small, with many repetitions at each step. First she was asked to view her genitalia in a mirror while she was by herself. This assignment ran counter to the old prohibitions against viewing and enjoying her body and, not surprisingly, made her extremely anxious. However, she eventually became comfortable with this and was then instructed to touch her genitals gently. She gradually became accustomed to this also and soon thereafter reported that she experienced pleasurable erotic sensations. Next she was told to place her finger into her vagina, which evoked intense anxiety and had to be repeated daily for two weeks. When Bridget could tolerate her own finger in her vagina, her husband was included in the assigned homework exercises and was most helpful. Initially, she was asked to insert her own finger into her vagina in his presence, which was followed by instructions for her to guide her husband's finger into her vaginal entrance. During the office sessions, the therapist carefully and clearly established that Bryan would allow her to maintain physical control over the speed, depth, and duration of the digital insertion. During the next phase of desensitization, he placed one finger deep into her vagina, still under her guidance and control. Later, two fingers were inserted.

---

* As a precaution against possible fetal damage, it is our practice to withhold medication for all patients prior to or during pregnancy, although I am not aware of any reports of tetralogy that has been attributed to antipanic medication.

The female superior position is usually used to complete the desensitization of penile penetration phobias because this gives the woman physical control over the speed, depth, and duration of penetration. Initially, the phobic woman is instructed to lower herself onto her husband's erect penis and stay there for a minute or two ("quiet vagina") while he lies still on his back. In subsequent sessions, Bridget gradually accustomed herself to slow, "non-demanding," up-and-down motions, and finally to thrusting to ejaculation. This goal was achieved at the twentieth session, in this case.

This patient's fears were intense and abated very slowly. But despite the considerable emotional discomfort she experienced each time she took a new step, she "stayed with" each exercise until her anxiety abated and the couple eventually succeeded in developing a normal sexual relationship. Bridget's ability to face and overcome her fears, her ardent wish for a child, her husband's love and support, and the power of the therapist's active encouragement which was amplified by her strong, positive "mother transference" to the therapist were all favorable factors in this case.*

Case Vignette #10: Emma

This patient was not particularly afraid of penetration, but had a specific aversion to breast stimulation. She avoided sexual intercourse with her husband primarily because of her fear that he might touch her breasts. She had no specific aversion to intromission and could tolerate this as long as it was rapid and she felt certain that her husband would refrain from caressing her breasts.

An entirely different behavioral sequence was required in this case.

It is a good idea to begin a desensitization program with sexual assignments that are already comfortable for the phobic patient as a starting point from which to expand his or her "sexual comfort zone."

The Sensate Focus exercises utilize this principle by commencing with non-erotic touching, which is fairly comfortable for patients with performance anxiety. But this was not appropriate in this

---

* Dr. Mildred Hope Witkin and her team treated this couple at the Payne Whitney Clinic.

case and the couple were told to have intercourse rapidly while the husband agreed to keep his hands away from the upper part of her body. They were already accustomed to this, but a small step towards desensitizing her "breast touching" phobia was introduced with the instruction that after coitus was complete she would take hold of his hand and place it lightly on her breast for one minute. She could stop him before the minute was up if she felt too tense.

She resisted this assignment, fearing that this would tempt him to exceed the limitations regarding breast contact. There was some basis in reality for her apprehension because he had on previous occasions "forgotten" that he had promised not to touch her breasts, a passive-aggressive expression of his rage about her "rules" and "rejections." This impasse provided an opportunity to begin to explore the couple's power struggle, which was an obstacle to improving their sexual relationship. Breast contact was prohibited until this issue was resolved in the office sessions. Then Emma gradually came to tolerate, and later to enjoy, her partner's caressing her breasts.

The Specific Phobic Stimulus

The specific phobic trigger is not always obvious and may be missed unless the evaluation is eclectic and considers the consciously perceived, unconscious and biological sources of the patient's sexual anxiety. The failure to identify its source accurately is a common cause of treatment failure that can often be traced to the "blind spot" created by the therapist's particular orientation and theoretical bias.

Analytically oriented therapists are not accustomed to interrupting their patients' accounts of their problems with direct questions in order to clarify the details of their current sexual behavior. If the patient does not volunteer this information, the analyst may fail to recognize a subtle phobic trigger. For instance, a man's phobic avoidance of having his partner see him without an erection, a secret which he cannot reveal to the "father" analyst, or a woman's revulsion by her husband's odor, which she is too embarrassed to mention, may escape the notice of a psychoanalyst who has spent years perfecting his ability to listen silently with his "third ear" for the deeper meaning of his patients' problems.

On the other hand, behavior therapists who are well trained in analyzing their patients' sexual behavior in precise detail may miss the critical point of intervention if the stimulus which evokes the phobic response is symbolically related to deeper neurotic processes and is not consciously recognized by the patient. For example, one of our patients with a sexual aversion who had failed to improve with behavioral sex therapy was phobic of and avoided women who reminded him of his mother. He could not report this to his therapist because he was not consciously aware of the connection. Not surprisingly, the standard SF exercises with his partner who resembled his mother failed to relieve his sexual anxiety.

Therapists who are not familiar with sexual panic states frequently fail to devise appropriate behavioral programs because they do not realize that the essential point of avoidance in these cases is often the patient's "fear of fear" and not his intrinsic fear of sex. These patients may avoid sex because they are apprehensive about panicking and losing control. This is the crucial issue which needs to be considered in structuring the therapeutic exposures.

The Emotional Impact of the Behavioral Assignments

The sexual interactions that are prescribed in sex therapy are not simply mechanical exercises. They are highly charged erotic and intimate experiences which the patient has previously avoided because they are too threatening to him. Although they are used by behavior therapists for the sole purpose of extinguishing the unwanted phobic response, in integrated sex therapy we also exploit the dynamic potential of the exposure assignments.

Behavioral prescriptions are extremely potent experiences that can rapidly strip away a patient's psychological defenses, and this can leave him feeling emotionally naked and vulnerable. While this is an excellent method for exposing important dynamic material and making this available for therapeutic exploration, the process can also be extremely threatening, especially in the context of conjoint therapy. For these reasons, the behavioral assignments should be devised with great sensitivity to their potential emotional effects on both spouses.

The therapist must understand the conscious as well as the unconscious meanings of the patient's sexual avoidance, and he should have a good idea about the impact the assignment is likely to make on the deeper neurotic processes that are shielded by the symptom. It will not do to construct a behavioral program only with desensitization in mind and without regard for its deeper psychodynamic ramifications. Ill-conceived assignments that tap too deeply into unconscious sexual conflicts or guilt may heighten the patient's anxieties to counterproductive levels and may mobilize intense resistances to the therapeutic process even though they are perfect in focus and intensity from a behavioral perspective.

In the worst scenario, sex therapy may precipitate aversive psychiatric reactions in patients whose egos are fragile (Kaplan, 1974). For example, my attempt to diminish Edith's phobic avoidance of sex by assigning an "intimate shower" (Witkin, 1982) with her husband, precipitated a major panic attack. The experience unlocked previously repressed memories of an incestuous incident which took place while she had showered with her older brother at the request of her hostile, manipulative mother (see p. 117).

Behavioral assignments can provoke crises that create valuable therapeutic opportunities. A crisis that taps into the patient's basic sexual conflict is a powerful technique for disrupting a resistant patient's defenses. We frequently deliberately precipitate therapeutically controlled crises when treatment stalls (Kaplan, 1979). But it serves no therapeutic purpose to assign behavioral exercises that create crises which are peripheral to the couple's sexual conflicts.

For example, exercises that involve self-stimulation can have substantial benefits in certain clinical situations. But for Orthodox Jews and devout Roman Catholics, masturbation is an anathema on religious grounds. Therefore, even though such an exercise might be correct from a behavioral perspective, the conflicts and guilts which the therapist's suggestion to masturbate are likely to evoke in deeply religious couples may nullify its therapeutic benefits. In addition, the therapist's insensitivity to the couple's value system can undermine their trust in him and endanger the therapeutic alliance which is such an extremely important ingredient in brief dynamic therapy.

When an assignment threatens to create an emotional crisis on account of issues which are peripheral to the patient's sexual problem, the potential detriment to the treatment process may outweigh its benefits and the therapist is well advised to seek an alternative treatment strategy.

Psychotherapists, psychoanalysts and behavior therapists are trained to focus on their individual patient's emotional needs and may neglect to consider the impact of their therapeutic interventions on his marriage. When working with these couples, the therapist must be especially careful that his assignments do not exert a destructive influence on their relationship. Behavioral prescriptions that stir up hostility between the partners or assignments that do not make partners look good to each other or are threatening to one of the partners are hardly likely to aid treatment. In psychodynamic sex therapy, all interventions must be devised with utmost sensitivity not only to the unconsciously expressed issues but to the unconscious dynamics of a couple's relationship as well.

Special sensitivity to the phobic partner's fear of abandonment and overreaction to rejection is required when working with couples where one partner has significant separation problems. These individuals are easily threatened by the process of therapy. They often fear that treatment may damage the relationship and the therapist's failure to tune in to this issue is a frequent cause of unnecessary treatment failure.

Individuals with separation problems often attempt to deal with their insecurities by developing an obsessive overconcern for their partners. They tend to put their own sexual needs aside in their compulsion to please. Assignments that interfere with these defenses may panic the individual and create crises fueled by their separation anxiety. Although this usually brings up extremely valuable material for the therapy sessions, the intensity of the patient's panic about losing the love or respect of his partner can disrupt the extinction process and cause the patient to flee from treatment.

For example, Frances, the phobic, anorgastic young woman, who was described in case #7 (page 55) found that assignments calling for her lover to pleasure her were extremely threatening.

A detailed analysis of the patient's current sexual behavior, revealed that Frances had become very skilled at arousing her lovers and giving them pleasure, while she phobically avoided receiving pleasurable erotic stimulation for herself. This was the immediate cause of her inability to climax.

She had developed a habit of removing only her underwear while making love, although she encouraged her partner to undress so she could caress and kiss him. She would usually bring him to orgasm orally, or, if he preferred to ejaculate intravaginally, she would arouse him and then make herself available for penetration. Frances' current lover, Frank, was uncomfortable with this situation. He had often expressed the desire to give her pleasure, and to help her have an orgasm, but she had never allowed him to do this.

Comfortable that the assignment would not antagonize or threaten Frank, I suggested that Frances take off her clothes and allow Frank to caress her genitalia for one minute before she was "allowed" to stimulate him. Frank was delighted with the assignment. Frances tried to comply, but panicked after Frank had touched her genitals for only a few seconds. She immediately yielded to her compelling desire to avoid the position of "receiver" and quickly stimulated him to orgasm instead.

The assignment had threatened Frances' obsessive "giving" which was a defense against her deep fears of being abandoned. This issue had to be dealt with before treatment could move forward.

I used this crisis to confront the patient with her excessive and irrational fears of rejection and loss, which were a distortion of reality. There was no reality basis for Frances' fear that Frank would leave her as he was obviously deeply in love with her. Her fears were clearly distortions from the past. We explored her painful childhood experiences. Frances' vulnerability to separation, which had been present since childhood, had been reinforced by repeatedly witnessing her mother's excruciatingly painful rejections by her promiscuous, seductive father. Although she was not consciously aware of this, Frances seemed to have determined that she would not allow herself to be exposed to hurt as her mother had been. At the same time she was deeply attracted to men who reminded her of her father.

Frances came to realize that she was setting herself up for problems by avoiding sexual arousal and orgasm and then becoming angry with her partners for depriving her. She also saw that this was meant to protect her against making herself vulnerable to the man. With these insights Frances began to make progress. She became more realistic in her appraisal of Frank's love for her and was beginning to enjoy sex with him. But shortly after she experienced her first orgasm with self stimulation, she accepted a position in a different city and abruptly left treatment. I believe that the patient's move represented a resistance to treatment. Even though she became orgastic, I regard this case as a treatment failure.

RESISTANCE

It is highly unusual to treat patients with sexual aversion disorders without encountering some resistance to the behavioral modification of their sexual avoidance. Resistances to treatment may be mounted by the sexually symptomatic patient or from her partner, and may be mobilized by the outcome as well as by the process of sex therapy. Resistances range in severity from mild and easily managed with simple support, encouragement, and minor modifications in the pace and intensity of the behavioral assignments to tenacious and complex, requiring great determination on the part of the therapist and also great expertise in brief psychodynamic and conjoint techniques.

Definition

Resistance has several meanings in the context of dynamic sex therapy. Resistance refers to the reluctance or refusal of patients or their partners to carry out their assignments. The term is also used when a patient is not open with the therapist during the sessions and withholds or distorts information. In the language of behaviorists, resistance denotes the failure of the patient's anxiety to diminish despite the fact that he has carried out the assigned desensitization tasks. And to the psycho-dynamically oriented clinician, the patient is resisting when he blocks or fails to remember significant dreams, memories, and associations, or when he "acts out" destructively outside the therapeutic setting.

The following lists some typical manifestations of resistance that may be encountered during the treatment of patients with sexual panic states.

1. *The patient missed the session because he/she:*
   a. forgot
   b. didn't feel well
   c. was too tired (either partner)
   d. was fighting with the partner
   e. had too many social activities
   f. masturbated compulsively
   g. had extramarital sex
   h. had a crisis in other aspects of life, e.g. fired from job, accident, etc.

2. *The patient sabotaged the sig* by:*
   a. doing the wrong assignment (misunderstood the directions)
   b. overdoing the assignment (anxiety level too high)
   c. underdoing the assignment (no anxiety)
   d. not "staying with" the assignment (aborting the experience before anxiety diminished)
   e. mentally detaching himself while doing the assignment (fantasized about irrelevant issues, tuned out)
   f. used C.N.S. depressant, alcohol, marijuana, etc. during the assignment
   g. put himself into a negative mental state while doing the assignment (obsessed about sexual performance, rejection)

3. *The patient did the assignment and improved, but spoiled the benefits by:*
   a. denying improvement, trivializing gains
   b. obsessing after successful assignment
   c. becoming depressed
   d. having an accident
   e. becoming ill

---

* Sig is the Latin term signa which we use to designate behavioral prescriptions in sex therapy.

    f. creating job problems
    g. developing other sexual symptoms
    h. developing other somatic symptoms

4. *The patient did not take medication and panicked because he/she:*
    a. forgot
    b. ran out of pills
    c. became "sick and tired" of medication
    d. overreacted to trivial side effects
    e. claimed to be feeling better: "I don't need the pills anymore."
    f. denied the beneficial effects

5. *The patient resisted in the office session by:*
    a. avoiding relevant material
    b. concealing important information
    c. bringing up diversionary topics, obsessing about irrelevant matters
    d. fighting with partner during session
    e. attacking the therapist or acting seductively with the therapist

Analyzing the Resistance

Each week's prescribed exercises should result in some noticeable improvement in the patient's aversion to or avoidance of sex, his insight into his deeper problems, and/or the quality of the couple's interactions. The absence of progress is pathognomic of resistance and treatment cannot proceed until the therapist understands where this is coming from and has devised effective counter measures.

We have found the following five questions, which are based on a multidimensional model of psychosexual pathology, useful for analyzing the resistance of patients and couples with sexual aversion disorders to sex therapy:

1. Are the behavioral assignments exposing the patient to the proper phobic stimulus? Are the intensity and pace of the extinction program conducive to extinction? Is the level of the patient's anxiety within an optimal therapeutic range?

2. Should the patient be given a trial of medication? Or if the patient already is on antipanic drugs, is he adequately medicated? Is he complying with his medication? Is he taking the right dose of the best drug?

3. Is the couple's resistance being mobilized by their conflicts about a successful *outcome* or by some aspect of the *process* of treatment? If so, what was threatening about last week's assignment? last week's interpretations?

4. Is the patient's failure to improve due to underlying sexual conflicts or guilt? Is the origin neurotic or cultural?
5. Are problems in the couple's relationship mobilizing resistance? Is the process of therapy or the sexual improvement threatening the partner? Is the resistance coming from the partner or from the symptomatic patient? Does either have panic disorder related to separation anxiety? Is therapy mobilizing the vulnerable partner's fear of abandonment?

Since partners often take turns resisting, continual attention to each spouse's reactions is needed to ascertain which one is sabotaging treatment at this point and why.

In the foregoing section, the importance of continually monitoring the behavioral assignments and adjusting these to ensure that the focus of the exposure is valid and that the extinction program is evoking an optimal level of anxiety has been discussed. When these potential behavioral sources of error in treatment have been reviewed and found faultless, and a review of the patient's medication indicates that he is being adequately protected against panics, and if it has been determined which partner is sabotaging treatment, we then shift to a psychodynamic formulation of psychosexual pathology and proceed on the assumption that the resistant partner's deeper unconscious conflicts are responsible for the treatment impasse.

During the initial evaluation of couples with sexual phobias and aversions, sufficient information should have been elicited about the culturally determined attitudes about sex which each partner had acquired during childhood, the dynamics of each partner's family, and the psychosexual development of each to enable the therapist to conceptualize the general outlines of the psychopathological infrastructure that lies beneath the couple's surface problem. In this way, the therapist will be prepared for the deeper emotional issues that are likely to emerge in the course of treatment and will be able to make inferences about the source and origins of the couple's resistances.* These can be tested and refined with the information provided by the weekly reviews of the couple's dreams, their mood, the quality of their relatedness to each other, and their attitude towards the therapist. When resistances emerge, it is then helpful to explore the patient's family history, his early significant relationships, and his sexual fantasies and their sources in greater detail until the crucial points of conflict become clear.

---

* The comprehensive assessment of sexual phobias and aversions and other sexual disorders is described in *The Evaluation of Sexual Disorders: Medical and Psychological Aspects* (Kaplan, 1983).

THE DYNAMIC ASPECTS OF TREATMENT

The emphasis on the behavioral aspects of treatment in the foregoing section may be misleading because actually the lion's share of the office visits are devoted to psychodynamic work. In reviewing the videotapes of our therapy sessions with sexually phobic and aversive patients, we found that on average 80 percent of our time was spent on dynamic exploration of the couple's resistances; only 20 percent was spent on reviewing their assigned experiences, working out their next behavioral sig, and assessing the patient's medication requirements.

Managing Neurotic Sexual Conflicts

The rapid modification of sexual symptoms that typically takes place during sex therapy and the relentless interference with neurotic and characterological defenses which the process often entails tend to mobilize anxiety and resistances in patients with neurotic conflicts about sex, as well as in their insecure partners. We attempt to deal with these kinds of resistances with brief active therapeutic interventions that are based on a psychodynamic model.

The clarification of underlying and unconscious intrapsychic and relationship problems assumes special importance in treating patients with panic disorders because medication alone does not resolve their deeper conflicts and defenses. We conduct the psychodynamic aspects of sex therapy with the assumption that the pathogenic effects of whatever childhood trauma they may have sustained might have been amplified because of their vulnerabilities. These individuals can ill afford to remain oblivious to the nature of their unconscious sexual conflicts and their neurotic relationship problems because these trouble them more deeply. Those who can develop keen insights into their unconscious and learn to recognize what triggers their excessive emotional reactions are in a much better position to protect themselves from emotional abuse and to develop successful love relationships and a good sex life.

However, a distinction must be drawn between such genuine insights into how their vulnerability to panic and their excessive separation anxieties have affected their psychosexual development and their object relationships and "insight" in the psychoanalytic sense. The latter is based on the assumption that a patient's understanding of previously repressed infantile trauma and the resolution of his childhood conflicts will cure his panics and separation problems.

Individuals with biologically normal capacities for anxiety who have separation problems may indeed become less anxious and their love relationships may improve when they attain insight through psychoanalysis into the problems they once experienced with their parents and siblings. However, if it proves to be true that patients with phobic anxiety syndrome have a biologically determined element of susceptibility to anxiety and separation problems, it would be a serious error to assume that this physiological abnormality can be altered by analysis of their early experiences. It is worse than useless, as well as frustrating, for both patient and analyst to engage in an exhaustive search for the psychological origins of their propensity to panic and for the psychic roots of their separation problems in patients who have a low panic threshold and a residual intolerance to separations on a constitutional basis. This hopeless quest keeps some individuals in expensive, discouraging, and useless analyses for years, continuing to be anxious while analysand and analyst remain convinced that if the patient could only "break through his resistance" and develop "genuine" insights into his preoedipal and oedipal problems, his pathological anxiety would abate.

Case Vignette #11: Rita

For example, Rita, one of our patients with an atypical panic disorder and a longstanding aversion to sex with the husband whom she loved and who loved her, was referred by her analyst. She had been in psychoanalysis with two well-known doctors for a total of 23 years (starting at age five) for her severe separation problems and her multiple phobias, which included a phobic avoidance of doctors, hospitals, and pregnancy.

In psychoanalysis the patient had traced her symptoms to the death of her beloved father when she was 11 years old. The feeling of abandonment had been aggravated by her stormy relationship with her narcissistic anxious mother.

This formulation was essentially valid as far as it went, but no consideration had ever been given to the patient's constitutional vulnerability which made the loss of her father doubly painful to her and the psychic damage much more serious and persistent.

Rita had adopted the psychoanalytic mystique, and on that account initially refused medication. In such cases, it is our practice to "join the patient's resistance." Thus, we began treatment without drugs. She made slow but steady progress in conjoint sex therapy with her husband until she panicked and relapsed at the thought that she would lose her therapist when treatment terminated. At this point, her sexual symptoms returned and she agreed to a trial of medication. We prescribed Norpramin 150 mgm. Fortunately, she was a good responder and was soon able to overcome her sexual aversion. She eventually separated herself successfully from her therapist and for the first time in her life developed close friendships with caring women of her own age. On follow-up one year after termination of treatment, the couple were still enjoying good sex and she was trying to become pregnant. She had not taken medication for six months.

Brief Dynamic Strategies in Sex Therapy

When unresolved problems from the past interfere with a patient's current sex life, the psychoanalyst will try to cure him by exploring and attempting to resolve his childhood conflicts. By contrast, the strategy in brief dynamic therapy is to attempt to find a way to *"bypass"* the patient's unresolved childhood conflicts and to free his current sexuality from the destructive influences of the past before resorting to lengthy reconstructive treatment.

For example, one of our patients, who had avoided sex with his wife for four years, was angry with, mistrustful of, and intimidated by women because he had never resolved his infantile ambivalent feelings towards his mother, whom he described as aggressive and demanding. He was really angry because his mother had preferred his father and her business to him. However, he defended himself with the fantasy that all women are angry, demanding, and unreasonable. This caused him to experience performance anxiety and erectile difficulties with his wife and ultimately led to his avoiding sex altogether.

In our experience with this kind of case, one is likely to get better and more rapid treatment results if one succeeds in modifying the immediate causes of the patient's sexual symptom directly with brief sex therapy methods rather than attempting to resolve his old Oedipal problems through psychoanalysis in the expectation that this will ultimately result in sexual improvement.

Although psychoanalytic theory predicts that this is not likely to happen, this patient, like many others, learned to overcome his performance anxiety and sexual avoidance. His image of his wife, who was really devoted to him, became more realistic although he still retained his infantile rage at his mother.

In our experience, only a small minority of patients who have more severe and compelling neurotic conflicts and personality disorders are unable to learn to sever the past from the present and need longer reconstructive treatment to improve their sexual functioning.

Dynamically Oriented Progressive Confrontation

Resistances that express the patient's neurotic sexual conflicts and/ or characterologic defenses are actively and relentlessly confronted as soon as they emerge. These confrontations and interpretations follow a progressively "deeper" course until the resistances are resolved.

We begin by interrupting the immediately operating surface defenses against sexual gratification which the patient consciously recognizes and then proceed to confront increasingly more threatening and deeply buried unconscious material until treatment moves forward again. At the same time, these active *confrontations* and interpretations are balanced with equally active relentless and empathic *support* of each partner and of their relationship (Kaplan, 1979).

The metaphor of "causal levels" rather than "causes" and the method of confronting these on progressively deeper levels have proved immensely useful for "bridging" over the deeper neurotic processes and conflicts which originally gave rise to the patient's psychosexual problem. This strategy minimizes divergence into areas of difficulty that are irrelevant for curing the patient's sexual symptom. This is an excellent discipline for keeping treatment as brief as possible. At the same time, the exploration of deeper material is not precluded when needed (Kaplan, 1979).

The couple's resistance to the exercises may bring to the surface their deeper sexual conflicts, guilts, and marital problems, tempting the therapist to stray away from the main therapeutic objective of sexual improvement. However, the exploration of pseudorelevant issues can play into the patient's resistances. For these reasons, it is a central principle of this approach that unconscious sexual conflicts, neurotic processes, and character traits *are never confronted unless they serve as a resistance to the treatment of the sexual problem.* As long as the patient's sexual anxieties and avoidances are steadily diminishing and the couple's intimacy and sexual pleasure together improving, the therapist does not bring up any extraneous material no matter how blatantly pathological it seems.

It is sometimes difficult for students with psychodynamically oriented backgrounds to focus on a couple's sexual improvement while leaving obvious but irrelevant psychopathology untouched. For example, in our videotaped continuous case seminar I treated a man with sexual panic disorder who had become quite obese since the couple's marriage. The trainees worried that the man's excessive weight gain was meant on an unconscious level to repel his wife and they wanted me to confront this issue. Yet I saw no evidence that his overeating served as a resistance

and, sticking to my discipline, I dealt only with the immediate causes
of this couple's sexual problem, his performance anxiety and her unreasonable sexual expectations. I never brought up his weight during
the sessions. I was lucky. The case was successfully concluded and the
trainees' anxieties were put to rest when, during the last session, the
young wife, with great emotion, told me how happy the success of
treatment had made her and how attractive she found her husband.

The irrational fear of sex and the phobic avoidance of sexual situations
are the specific and immediate causes of sexual panic states. But other
immediately operating obstacles to sexual functioning, notably performance panic and obsessive overconcern for the partner, are often con-
tributing elements to the patient's avoidance of sex. Immediate causes
of sexual symptoms cannot be bypassed. Unless these are modified, the
patient cannot improve. The immediate antecedents of the couple's
sexual avoidance are treated directly with behavioral techniques; it is
only when the patient resists the behavioral modification of the destructive mental processes which are currently maintaining the symptom
that treatment shifts into a dynamic mode.

The dynamic aspects of treatment are active and direct, guided by
the therapist's conceptualization of the neurotic infrastructure of the
phobic patient's sexual symptoms and of the couple's pathological interactions. Therefore, the therapist needs to have an in depth understanding of both partners' psychodynamics and psychosexual development, although in most cases only a fraction of this material will be
dealt with explicitly during treatment.

The following treatment fragment may convey the flavor of the brief,
dynamic strategies we use in the treatment of patients with sexual
aversion disorders.

Case Vignette #12: Ernie and Edith

The couple had been referred by the wife's psychoanalyst for
their sexual avoidance, which had begun 17 years before on their
honeymoon. Prior to the wedding, they had enjoyed good sex
together. Both had been in individual therapy for 17 years because
of this problem, with no improvement of their sexual relationship.

Her analyst had diagnosed Edith as having a borderline personality disorder. We also found "soft signs" of an (atypical) panic
disorder. She had a history of school avoidance and several phobias
apart from the phobic element in her sexual avoidance.

Ernie, apart from a long-standing tendency to sabotage his career success and some passive-aggressive traits, had no major psychological problems.

During the sixth session, the couple reported that they had not done their SF II exercises, giving the usual excuses (the children interfered, they were too busy, etc.). I accepted their rationalizations, and also confronted their anxiety about facing their sexual difficulties in a supportive, nonjudgmental manner. I repeated the assignment and, to make it more comfortable for this phobic woman, I asked the husband to take responsibility for initiating the exercises that week.

They came in the next week without having done the assignments.

One immediate cause of the couple's long-standing sexual avoidance had been the refusal of each to initiate sex. She was too vulnerable to risk rejection. He was reluctant to approach her because her anxiety put him off so that he was afraid that he would not be able to function. But I was not yet certain about the deeper causes.

Nothing would happen unless I could get past their avoidance. I confronted their resistance more strongly, this time not accepting the excuses. I told them that I understood that this was difficult for them but they would not improve unless they could do the assignments. Ernie told me that he may not "be ready" for sex therapy. I told him that after 17 years of psychotherapy he was as ready as he ever would be.

I thought he might be ambivalent about the marriage, possibly because of her anxiety and nongiving narcissistic attitude or possibly because he had an intrinsic commitment conflict. That would explain his choice of a woman with Edith's emotional problems for his wife.

I repeated the assignment, designating two specific times in order to "bypass" the resistance of "who takes the first step." I also asked to see each separately next time so as to explore the deeper causes of their resistances.

The following week they managed to do their SF II exercise once.

In the session alone with Ernie I found that my hunch was wrong. It turned out that he was not ambivalent about commitment to the marriage, nor was he thinking of leaving Edith. He had fantasies of a warm family life and he really wanted to make his marriage work. He revealed another immediate obstacle to good sex. He had avoided using his erotic fantasies when he was with his wife. They involved having sex with black women and with women wearing "whorish" underwear. He had not been aware that on an unconscious level he was guilty about his fantasies and felt that he must make a choice between "clean," married "lovemaking" and "getting laid" with "dirty" women. This was a residue of his puritanical upbringing and could also have involved some unresolved Oedipal problems. I confronted this resistance, reconceptualized his distorted views of married sexual life and gave him "permission" to have both. I suggested that he use his favorite fantasy while his wife stimulated him. My message was: "It's OK to have "dirty" (i.e., passionate) sex with your wife."

In my sessions with Edith it became apparent that she was anxious and guilty about being sexy and attractive to men. She became panicky when Ernie wanted sex and she had phobically avoided the role of a sexually desirable woman. She did not trust women. In our sessions without him we explored the origins of this pattern of sexual self-sabotage, which could be traced to her destructive relationship with her manipulative mother. Edith had been an anxious youngster emotionally dependent on her mother. The mother was a narcissistic competitive woman, who did not encourage her daughter's sexual development and who interfered with her relationship with her father. I proceeded on the assumption that the vulnerable little girl had internalized her mother's negative messages that she was not entitled to be a sexual winner. This gave rise to her unattractive manner and appearance which was the immediate obstacle to treatment. In addition to exploring these issues further, I attempted to provide a corrective experience.

I told her that, even if this made her anxious, if she wanted Ernie to make love to her, she must stop going to bed in a sweatsuit. I asked her to buy an attractive nightgown before next week's session. I pointed out that her husband loved her but that any man would be put off by her anxious, negative responses to his sexual advances.

The behavioral aspect of treatment proceeded to engage the couple in progressively more intense physical and psychic erotic stimulation. I made no further interpretations until I assigned an "intimate shower" (Witkin, 1982). This caused the wife to have a serious panic attack.

The assignment had evoked deeply buried, incestuous fantasies of having sex in the shower with her father, which were "screened" by memories about incestuous experiences in the shower with her brother. My suggestion heightened her suspiciousness towards me which grew out of her mother transference to me. Her ambivalence towards me created an obstacle which I had to deal with if treatment was to go forward.

I tuned into her painful childhood experiences. Together, with great compassion, we explored the implications of her vulnerability on her development. She came to see that because of her sensitivities, she was probably much more hurt by her mother than a more placid child would have been.

In sessions alone together we discussed how her rage toward her mother had intensified her guilt about her fantasies of seducing her father. As a result, she was still afraid to make it with her husband. She understood her father transference to Ernie intellectually, but her sexual anxiety did not abate.

Her phobic sexual avoidance anxiety was an obstacle that would not yield to behavioral modification. I decided to try to provide a corrective experience for her by modeling appropriate female behavior. In the next conjoint session I was especially warm and sensitive to Edith. She responded immediately and enthusiastically. I was the "good mother" and I wanted to make it clear that, unlike her real mother, I wanted her to copy the way I acted so *she* could win the attention and love of her handsome husband. She began to believe that I was on her side and started to identify with me. I showed her and told her that I *wanted* her to have the man. "Ernie is not your father, you are entitled to be happy with him." I asked him to take her to her favorite restaurant and to "court" her this week. So that *he* wouldn't feel rejected, I made it clear that next week it would be her turn to do the same for him. I asked her to respond honestly and, if possible, positively to any sexual advance he might make. She was "allowed" to say "This makes me anxious," but she was "not allowed" to act in a negative avoidant manner.

The next week she looked remarkably more attractive. The couple had had good sex.

There were still many unconscious neurotic processes we had not discussed within the context of this brief treatment, and we might never do so. However, I had dealt with her unconscious conflicts deeply enough to "bypass" her immediate defenses against sex. She was able to identify with me and risk behaving seductively and making him feel wanted. He responded sexually and emotionally. She was reassured by my enthusiastic approval. But Edith continued to avoid sex. At this point I suggested a trial of medication. Unfortunately, the patient did not respond. But we persisted and very slowly her phobic avoidance of sex diminished.

Sometime later in treatment Ernie became depressed. Despite the obvious improvement in the couple's sexual relationship, he told me that he was pessimistic: "I feel that I will never have an erection again." The resistance was not coming from Edith who had clearly become more sensitive, supportive, and encouraging.

I now had to deal with Ernie's resistance. Progressively I confronted his fear of success. When this did not resolve the resistance, we went to his guilt about being his mother's favorite and "doing better" than his father and brother. I did not, however, delve into the oedipal material. Instead I used shared fantasies to help the couple "bypass" his "madonna-whore" splitting of intimate and erotic relationships.

Treatment progressed. Neither had worked through their deeper conflicts. But the quality of their relationship improved, they learned to cope with her insecurities and with his performance anxiety, and they had fairly pleasurable sex every week or so.*

Within this basic conceptual theme, an endless variety of verbal as well as experiential techniques can be used. *The technical variations depend on the emotional needs of the couple and on the therapist's style and creativity.*

For example, to resolve a treatment impasse, we may create a therapeutically controlled crisis—by joining the resistance, or by strong, deep confrontations during the office sessions, or by assigning paradoxical interactions as homework.

Thus, one patient whose resistance to sex took the form of hypercriticalness towards her husband was instructed to observe carefully the interactions between herself and him. If he did or said anything that had the slightest negative implication or if he showed any lack of sensitivity to her feelings, she was to refuse to have any physical contact with him for a whole week. The ridiculousness of the assignment forced her to own up to her sexual fears and to acknowledge that she was using her excessive criticisms as an excuse to avoid sex with her husband.

When conducting sexual therapy with sexually phobic individuals, regardless of whether or not they are medicated, and regardless of whether or not they respond, it is especially important to confront distortions and resistances that arise from the separation problems and

---

* Both remained in their individual therapies and continued to work on these problems after the termination of sexual therapy.

overreaction to criticism typical of patients with panic disorders. These patients need to understand that their tendencies to overreact and misinterpret the partner's behavior as rejecting is likely to alienate and infuriate him, and that making one's partner angry is a highly effective avoidance mechanism.

These vulnerable patients can also permit their excessive feelings of rejection to provide a defense against letting themselves feel sexual pleasure. We confront this kind of resistance very directly. An individual whose agitation about his wife's lack of "openness" is ruining their sex life together may be told, for example, that in the therapist's opinion he is misreading his wife's sexual response; that her not having orgasm during coitus does not mean that she does not love him; and that his obsession about mutual orgasm is self destructive, upsets her, and maintains his sexual avoidance.

Support

The emphasis on confrontation in the preceding section should not be taken to imply that the treatment process is harsh or inhuman, or that the therapist is supposed to act like a drill sergeant. To the contrary. This brief, active, dynamic method requires an extremely strong therapeutic alliance and the relentless confrontations are not effective unless they are balanced with equally consistent and equally "relentless" support of both partners and of their relationship. The couple must sense that the therapist only pursues these tough confrontations so relentlessly, because she is deeply committed to helping them.

Again, the process of sex therapy can make couples feel extremely vulnerable. They are both asked to expose their most sensitive secrets to the strange doctor and to each other. They are confronted with their inner fears and wishes and are rapidly divested of defenses which have protected them for a long time. They are asked to engage in highly charged, erotic experiences which they have never been able to risk before because they are too threatening. The woman, who is exquisitely sensitive about her small breasts and has always kept them covered, faces a crisis when she is told that she is supposed to allow her lover to slowly caress her nude body in a revealing light. The man, who has phobically avoided letting a woman see him without an erection on account of his agonizing obsession that his penis is too small, finds the Sensate Focus exercises, which entail exposing himself to her eyes and her hands in a flaccid state, extremely threatening.

No couple, and most especially not those with panic disorder related vulnerabilities, can take such risks unless each feels understood, supported and safe with the therapist, and unless they have confidence in his competence. This requires that the therapist be truly skilled, experienced, and secure in his knowledge and technical expertise. Also, to excel at this kind of treatment, the therapist must be extremely sensitive and possess the capacity for genuine empathy. He must be able to feel and to "stay with" their pains, fears, anxieties, and vulnerabilities. But it is equally important for him to be able to empathize, "stay with" and enjoy the couple's pleasure and sexual gratification. He must be able to feel genuinely supportive of their commitment to each other.

Managing Cultural Guilts About Sex

Patients whose sexual phobias and aversions can be traced primarily to their families' negative attitudes about sex are generally easier to treat than those with neurotic sexual conflicts who are more likely to have more serious emotional problems. Cultural and neurotic sexual conflicts both fall into the category of "remote" causes in the sense that both originated long ago in the patient's childhood, but we conceptualize cultural and neurotic causes differently and we use somewhat different treatment strategies.

The resolution of cultural sexual problems depends more on the therapist's support and "permission" to enjoy erotic pleasure than on the progressive method of confronting resistances which is our main weapon against neurotic sexual conflicts. The sexual guilt that is carried by persons who were taught as children that sex is sinful, dangerous, and disgusting often gives rise to resistance to a therapy that is designed to enhance their sexual pleasure. These individuals often remain uncomfortable with their sexual feelings, still having the sense that sex is somehow dirty and wrong. They are often conflicted about pleasure and may feel guilty about enjoying the sexual exercises. They also tend to feel irrationally guilty about a successful treatment outcome. The therapist's support of their "sexual rights" and her encouragement to enjoy erotic pleasure are keys to the successful treatment of these cases.

We confront the resistances that grow out of cultural sexual guilt as soon as they arise, just as we do with resistances that have neurotic sources. But in these cases we try to *expose* the early roots of the sexual conflict to the compassionate light of reason, rather than to make an attempt to *bypass* these.

Patients whose sexual aversions derive from their antisexual upbringing must become conscious of their irrational guilt about sexual pleasure and they need to attain insight into its malignant effects. Therefore, in therapy we immediately and with sympathetic understanding review the negative messages about sex that the patient received from his family and connect these directly to his current difficulty. We point out that when a person is brought up with old-fashioned or religious restrictive sexual attitudes it is very difficult to change gears suddenly later in life, even though it is O.K. to have sex now that she is married. Interpretation that they are still victimized by their early antisexual programming makes sense to these patients and is not ordinarily threatening. In fact, patients with cultural guilt about sex and sexual pleasure anxiety are often relieved by the therapist's message that sex is a natural function which everyone is entitled to and by her "permission" to enjoy sexual pleasure.

A therapist's compassionate formulation of the special difficulties that strict prohibitions against masturbation or against premarital sex can cause for the person with panic disorder related emotional vulnerabilities can be extremely liberating for these individuals.

Sexual pleasure anxiety and guilt are absolute obstacles to sexual improvement in these cases and freeing the patient from sexual guilt is a major objective of treatment. The therapist's task of liberalizing the patient's cruel conscience and diminishing his harsh self-judgments can be facilitated by using therapeutic techniques that encourage the patient to identify with the therapist and to adopt her more permissive sexual values. The process of identification is more readily achieved if the therapist projects an attractive, professional image that patients can look up to. The message that "sex is O.K." is not likely to be "heard" if it comes from an unprofessional individual whom the couple does not admire.

Modeling appropriate communication skills and attractive gender-appropriate demeanor can be an effective therapeutic maneuver for helping patients overcome their avoidance of sexual success. Some female patients (Edith, p. 115) were never encouraged, or were even actively discouraged, by their mothers, to learn how to feel and behave like attractive, sexually competent women. A trusted female therapist can provide an important corrective experience.

The insecure male has a similar opportunity to identify with a sexually competent, encouraging male therapist. These therapeutic experiences supply the missing parental approval and provide effective role models which are important ingredients in normal psychosexual development. These techniques can often shortcircuit the necessity for lengthy explorations and resolution of the patient's destructive relationship with the same gender parent.

Well-controlled *self-disclosures* that permit patients to catch glimpses of the therapist's personal life can facilitate a positive identification with the therapist and her values. Self-disclosure can be very useful in sex therapy, but this is also potentially hazardous because inappropriate intimacy with patients that grows out of the therapist's unrecognized neurotic emotional needs is always destructive. However, when this is skillfully done by a therapist who has sufficient insights into his own motives to insure that he is not acting out of his uncontrolled sexual or exhibitionistic or competitive needs, the therapist's self-disclosures can provide a corrective model and facilitate the rapid development of a less punitive and more flexible and rational conscience or superego.

For example, the therapist might say *to a patient of the same gender:* "Most people have sexual fantasies, even your boss, your housekeeper, your kids, and myself."

Benefits: Gives permission for and models enjoyment of erotic fantasies.
Risks: Potentially seductive or competitive.

The therapist might say *to a patient of the opposite gender:*

Female therapist to male patient: "But a woman wouldn't expect a man to have an instant erection every time. I certainly don't expect my husband to."
Male therapist to female patient: "My wife certainly wouldn't expect me to."

Benefits: Models realistic and supportive behavior for wife; reduces man's performance anxiety; gives man permission to defend himself against partner pressure.
Risks: Evoking competitive feelings (I would be a better sexual partner for her than you are; or my wife is a better sexual partner than yours).

The therapist might say *to a patient of the same gender:*

Female therapist to female patient: "I was also afraid (or embarrassed) by (oral sex, masturbating, having an orgasm, etc.) in the beginning."
Male therapist to male patient: I was also afraid I would come too fast (or stay erect, didn't know how women had orgasms) when I started.

Benefits: gives permission and models that it is okay to be vulnerable.
Risks: evoking competitive feelings (I'm way ahead of you sexually); potentially seductive.

Therapists who have themselves experienced or been close to someone with panic disorder related difficulties are often unusually gifted and effective in working with these patients. The therapist might say to the panicky partner: "I know just how you feel. I also used to let my rejection sensitivity get the best of me, upset me, etc."

Benefits: Raises patient's self-esteem; gives couple hope that things can change.
Risks: Making partner feel left out, manipulated.

The therapist who has established a trusting relationship with his sexually anxious patient is in an excellent position to use her evoked feelings to detect and help him correct his subtly destructive interpersonal behavior. For example, if a patient is too demanding and obsessive and pressures the therapist during the sessions, she can tell him how uncomfortable he makes her feel and point out that she hopes that this is not the way he acts with his partner in a sexual situation, because any woman might be alienated and offended by this kind of behavior no matter how attractive she finds him.

The therapist dealing with patients with phobic anxiety syndrome needs to maintain his sensitivity to their vulnerabilities and his empathic connection with their anxieties during the vicissitudes of the treatment process. He should be able to genuinely identify with their painful struggle to overcome their anxieties, but at the same time it is crucial that the therapist avoid adopting an overprotective attitude towards his vulnerable patients. If he is to help them cope with their sexual anxieties, and if he is to succeed in teaching them how to make themselves comfortable with their partners, the therapist must remain constructively realistic and have the emotional strength to set appropriate and consistent limits. It is extremely important in working with these needy, obsessive patients to remain relentlessly fixed on the treatment goal of improving their sexual functioning and their romantic relationships; otherwise, therapy can become diverted into endless peripheral issues which serve only to perpetuate the patient's maladaptive behavior and avoidance of sex.

CHAPTER 6

The Couple With Sexual Panic Disorder: Separation Anxiety and Conjoint Sex Therapy

Excessive separation anxiety is a distinctive feature of phobic-anxiety syndrome. But apart from the complications that can arise from their special vulnerability to *separation, rejection,* and *criticism* from the person they love, these individuals exhibit the same diversity in their object relationships that we see in persons with a normal panic threshold.

Some men and women with panic disorder have serious personality deficits and lack the ability to enter into mature, mutually gratifying love relationships. Others can love but develop marital problems because they form neurotic parental transferences towards their sexual partners. Many have a perfectly normal capacity for love and commitment, even though they are oversensitive to separations.

The fit that these individuals work out with their partner is extremely important in determining the quality of their romantic relationships. Some persons with panic disorder related separation problems find partners who truly love and accept them and who are sensitive to their emotional needs. They establish wonderfully close and loving relationships. Marital problems are not material in the pathogenesis of sexual difficulties if these should occur in such a couple. Treatment can proceed directly to the extinction of the symptomatic partner's sexual phobia or aversion.

However, the vulnerable partner's separation anxiety related problems frequently give rise to pathological interactions and ambivalences which constitute the primary causes of the couple's sexual difficulties. Individuals who are overly sensitive to rejection may alienate their partners with their excessive emotional demands. Others have problems in their marriages because of their defensive avoidance of intimacy and commitment. When such "pathological interlocks" create obstacles to the extinction of the symptomatic partner's phobic avoidance of sex, this becomes the first issue that must be addressed in treatment.

Of course, persons who do not suffer from panic disorder can also develop pathological separation anxiety on a purely psychogenic basis and they experience similar marital problems. Many of the separation anxiety related issues in conjoint sex therapy that are described in this chapter pertain equally to couples with or without a biological propensity for these problems. However, there are some particular kinds of marital difficulties which are related to the presumably physiological and drug-responsive separation problems of these couples that are significant from a clinical perspective.

Our therapeutic approach to resistances generated by relationship problems is a conjoint version of the brief dynamic method we use for intrapsychic neurotic resistance, and is based on similar premises (p. 113).

We actively support both partners and their commitment to the relationship. First we attempt to modify the immediate sources of friction between them, "bypassing" hidden, threatening relationship issues as much as possible. Therefore, the partner's individual problems are *not* confronted, reconceptualized or interpreted, no matter how blatant these seem, if they are not causing problems in the couple's relationship nor mobilizing resistances to treatment.

But we confront resistances that are destructive to the couple's sexual relationship *as soon as* these surface and we pursue these *relentlessly on a progressively deeper and more defended level of conscious awareness until the obstacle to treatment is resolved.* If either partner's separation anxiety is material in their sexual and/or marital problem, we clarify and actively confront this issue.

Patients and couples with panic disorder related problems often find the therapist's reconceptualization of the syndrome illuminating and helpful. But in a conjoint session, such explanations must be done with great sensitivity. The word "panic" often has negative implications. The idea that the doctor sees a spouse as "sick" or "weak" can be extremely threatening to both partners.

The following fragment of the treatment of a couple with bilateral sexual avoidance, which was complicated by the husband's panic disorder, will illustrate how we conceptualize separation anxiety related problems in conjoint sex therapy.

Case Vignette #13: Norman and Norma

Norman, age 65, had recently retired as a senior partner in a successful law firm. He had been married for four years to Norma, a noted artist who was 50 years old.

During the first two years of their marriage, they had enjoyed a passionate sexual relationship, but gradually the frequency of their sexual encounters had declined. When I first saw them, they had not made love in eight months. Norman also complained that Norma had grown distant and disinterested in other ways as well.

There was an obsessive quality to the husband's need for his wife's attention, which we often see in relationships where one partner has excessive separation anxiety. Norman had a panic disorder, with occasional bouts of mild spontaneous panic attacks, mitral valve prolapse, a fear of heights, and a tendency to overreact to rejection and criticism. Otherwise, he was a highly functional, well integrated person who deeply loved his wife.

Norma was free of major psychopathology. She reciprocated Norman's love, but she was also deeply committed to her painting. She did not handle her husband's distress and anger about her dual commitment well, partially because she did not understand his inherent sensitivity and also because of her own problems.

The couple came into the office reporting that their fights about when they would do the SF exercises had prevented them from carrying out the assignment. Norman had been complaining for some time that Norma rose very early every morning to paint, but that this was when he liked to make love. She had explained that she must work in the early morning because that was when her creativity was at its peak, but she had repeatedly told him that she would be happy to make love to him at any other time. This was unacceptable to him and he felt rejected and angry. She felt frustrated and pressured.

Their struggle about when to do their sexual homework was clearly the immediate obstacle to treatment. I first attempted to "bypass" their resistance by helping them negotiate a reasonable compromise. I took the position that she was certainly entitled to pursue her art career and that he had a right to expect love and companionship in his marriage. But I also confronted them with the fact that if they were going to fight about this, treatment would not work. Moreover, neither was getting what he or she wanted; she was not painting and he was not feeling loved.

I tried to get them to deal with the problem realistically. We discussed the fact that the morning had always been the most productive time for her, long before she met him. I pointed out that many artists do their best work before the pressures of the day interrupt their thoughts and that her habit of painting in the morning was not a rejection of him. But I also attempted 'to get her to see that his desire for morning sex was not just a means of bullying her. I explained that men at his age function best in the early morning on a physical basis and that it was quite natural that he would want sex at that time.

They arrived at a compromise that they would do the SF exercises on Sunday and Wednesday and Friday mornings and that she would paint on Monday, Tuesday, Thursday and Saturday.

If this had worked, no further exploration of their relationship would have been required and we could have proceeded with the behavioral modification of their sexual avoidance.

But the resistance of couples whose sexual problems are associated with significant separation problems can seldom be bypassed this easily. Their feelings are often too intense, negotiations break down, and it becomes necessary to deal with the deeper problems that lie concealed beneath such apparently trivial issues as the wife's work habits.

In this case, the husband could not contain his smouldering rage. His wife's involvement with her work had tapped into old feelings of pain and anger about having been slighted and "ignored" by his career-oriented mother. He developed insomnia and behaved irritably and badly towards Norma all week. She was so distressed by his anger that she couldn't paint and she became depressed. His disapproval activated her old unresolved guilt about putting her own needs before those of others.

I proceeded on the theory that they were stuck at this point because neither understood the hidden issue of Norman's separation anxiety and I decided to clarify this issue.

For these relationships to work, both must face and accept the reality of the partner's emotional make-up and they both need to develop insight into the destructively spiraling impact that the one's tendency to overreact to separations and rejections and the other's defensive response have on their communications and on their relationship.

During the next session I discussed Norman's separation anxiety with the couple in the most positive terms I could think of. We explored the possibility that Norman's sensitivity had made his mother's commitment to her career especially painful for him as a child. We also began to look at what his overreaction to rejection was doing to his relationship with Norma.

But verbal explanations alone may not suffice to get this concept across constructively, unless this is reinforced by the therapist's active support of the patient and of the relationship.

The therapist should persist in reassuring the partner who is oversensitive to rejection that his spouse really loves him, until he "hears" this. It also helps to consistently confront distortions or exaggerated feelings of hurt or anger arising from his emotional vulnerabilities. Of course, these tactics are appropriate only if this is true. But when it is, the therapist's unremitting support and her expressions of faith in the viability of the relationship are powerful ingredients in the successful treatment of these couples.

The therapist's gentle patience in dealing with their intense need for reassurance also models constructive behavior for the spouse. I made it a point during our conjoint sessions to express my compassion when he described the painful feelings of rejection he experienced whenever she seemed to put her work ahead of him. But I also expressed understanding and sympathy for her feeling oppressed by his pressuring and angered by his cavalier attitude towards her work.

When working with couples with sexual panic disorder in a conjoint mode, the therapist must try to impart constructive and realistic attitudes to the vulnerable partner and support his right to make himself comfortable without threatening the other one. The therapist's admiration for what the patient has accomplished despite his problems enhances his image with his wife, while at the same time encouraging him to develop a sense of pride in his ability to cope. The therapist's message that his rejection sensitivity and his need for an extra caring and sensitive partner are no reflection on his manhood also serves to strengthen the relationship.

Partners of rejection-sensitive individuals have to be helped to learn not to be overwhelmed by their anxious partner's needs nor intimidated by their anger. They must learn to take care of themselves without guilt, while at the same time maintaining their sensitivity to their partner's needs.

In the conjoint sessions with Norman and Norma, we discussed how difficult it is for many couples to work out a comfortable balance when the husband expects an exclusive commitment from his wife who has a *dual* commitment to her career and to the marriage.

I tried to get them to see that Norman's pain and his fury at feeling that he was playing second fiddle to his wife's work were the result of many forces. These included his inherent sensitivity to rejections and the fact that Norma's behavior had tapped into his old pain and anger that his mother had loved her work better than him. Moreover, these issues had all been intensified by his recent retirement.

Norma finally "heard" how deeply wounded her husband felt when she left his morning embrace to pursue her own interests and Norman began to realize that he was setting himself up for a devastating rejection.

By interfering with her attempts to balance her career and her marriage and by putting her in the position of having to choose between her love for her art and her love for him, he was making it impossible for her to respond to him. If she tried to comply with his request to give up her best painting time in order to make love to him, she would feel trapped and much too angry and the relationship would deteriorate.

Norman and Norma loved each other, neither was emotionally disturbed, and their relationship was basically sound. It was therefore possible to help them improve their difficulties by bringing out the hidden separation anxiety related issue, and it was not necessary to use medication to cure this couple's sexual avoidance. In order to resolve the therapeutic impasses of couples whose sexual aversions are associated with more serious neurotic marital interactions, it often becomes necessary to work more extensively with more deeply buried material, to confront the spouses' destructive parental transferences towards one another, and to use medication.

Marital problems that grow out of the spouses' parental transferences towards each other tend to be particularly intense and dramatic in couples with sexual panic disorders. However, as long as they are basically committed to one another, it is often possible to bypass these neurotic processes successfully within the context of brief conjoint sexual therapy.

The prognosis is poor with sexual therapy when sexual panic states are associated with more serious psychopathology and severe marital problems. The following case vignette illustrates a treatment failure in a couple with long-standing marital problems, bilateral sexual dysfunctions, and a severe personality disorder associated with panic disorder on the part of the wife.

Case Vignette #14: Alice and Alan

Alan, an attractive, cultured stockbroker, age 60, presented with a complaint of primary premature ejaculation (PE). He and Alice, who was 59 years old, had been married for 38 years, and had one daughter.

Alice, who was an obese but attractive woman, had a severe aversion to and avoidance of sex with her husband. She attributed this to his poor ejaculatory control. She typically became anxious and panicky when Alan indicated that he wanted to make love to her and would then berate him furiously for his "sexual inadequacy" and his "passive-aggressiveness." Alice met the criteria for borderline personality disorder and also reported that she had experienced spontaneous panic attacks during several periods in her life. She was extremely dependent on, but highly ambivalent and abusive towards her husband. She was crippled by anxiety when he was away, but constantly attacked, belittled, and criticized him when they were together. The wife felt anxious and insecure unless she exerted total emotional and sexual control over her husband.

Alan was a passive, neurotic individual who was locked into the marriage by his own separation problems.

The wife had been in analysis for 16 years, and the husband had seen a therapist for five years, with no improvement of their sexual or marital relationship.

I initially attempted to treat the couple's bilateral sexual problem in conjoint sexual therapy, but her panicky response to sexual arousal and her unremitting rage at him made this impossible.

Alice was medicated and I saw her individually, while Alan was seen by another therapist in our group in an attempt to prepare them for sex therapy.

Alice's father had been an emotionally distant figure who died when she was eight. Her mother, who was still living, was a disturbed, sadistic woman who was subject to violent outbursts of temper, during which she had periodically abused the patient physically and emotionally during her childhood. Alice had never resolved her ambivalent attachment to her mother. She treated her own daughter and also her husband in an ambivalent, abusive, and intrusive manner, which echoed her pathological interactions with her mother.

After a year of therapy and medication (Tofranil 250 mgm.), Alice's sexual anxiety had diminished sufficiently so that she could now enjoy masturbating to orgasm. Her mood lifted and she became much more comfortable and successful at her job. But there was no improvement in the couple's marriage nor in her sexual relationship with Alan.

I again attempted conjoint sex therapy. Alan was cooperative and his ejaculatory control improved, but Alice continued to panic, to avoid the assignments, and to sabotage treatment by violently berating her husband.

Miraculously, the couple managed to enjoy two mutually pleasurable sexual experiences where he maintained ejaculatory control and she was orgastic. But she immediately reverted back to her rage at him and to her sexual avoidance, which she now blamed on his insufficient earning power. He never learned to defend himself.

This case was a treatment failure. On follow-up one year later, the couple had had successful sex together only twice and their relationship had not changed.

THE PARTNER

Partner engagement is extremely important in the treatment of sexually aversive patients with separation problems because these overly sensitive individuals are especially vulnerable to the subtlest negative nuances from their lovers. The situation is similar when the sexually asymptomatic partner has separation problems. Insecure partners, especially those with significant separation sensitivities, are apt to feel threatened by their spouse's sexual improvement. In these cases, the therapist must exercise the utmost sensitivity to their fears about being rejected or else they are likely to sabotage treatment. We have sometimes found it helpful to medicate rejection-sensitive, sexually asymptomatic *partners* with panic disorders who become intensely anxious during the successful treatment of their spouse's sexual disorders. Medication can be discontinued after the partner's sexual functioning has improved and after the vulnerable partner is convinced her now sexually adequate spouse won't leave her.

Sexual Aversion in the Partner of the Anxious Spouse

Alan (Case Vignette #14) endured abuse from Alice for years without losing his sexual interest in her. In fact no other woman had ever attracted him, and he had never had another sexual partner. It may be speculated that on an unconscious level Alice fulfilled his erotic fantasy of having a dominant, cruel, and powerful mother permit him to have sex with her. But unless this plays into their masochistic fantasies, most persons are repelled by an anxious partner's excessive emotional demands and by their anger when they are frustrated.

The insecurities of the person with separation problems are heightened, sometimes to obsessive proportions, when he senses that his partner is not completely "with him." Under such circumstances, his anxious, obsessive quest for reassurance can precipitate sexual avoidance in a partner with normal separation responses. In such cases, the (sexually) asymptomatic partner's obsessive behavior is the immediate cause of the couple's sexual problem and this must be modified in treatment.

An individual with separation problems may become so obsessed with pleasing his partner that he interferes with her sexual pleasure by anxiously checking out her response to see if she is lubricated or by expressing intense dismay should she fail to have an orgasm. If she does have an orgasm, he insists on a detailed description of her experience. During sex therapy, after a successful Sensate Focus experience, the anxious partner sometimes spoils the relaxed and intimate mood by excessively "affectionate" and clinging behavior and by pressing his partner to "communicate" and reassure him that she truly enjoyed it. One patient with an underlying panic disorder, who had a sexual aversion associated with transvestitism, became both euphoric and anxious when he felt emotionally and physically close to his wife for the first time in his life after the Sensate Focus exercises. He followed her around the house all week, constantly hugging and kissing her. Not suprisingly, the wife felt a compelling urge to go to Arizona to visit her mother and to escape from treatment until this issue was clarified during the next therapy session. She had been afraid to say "no" to him, fearing she would traumatize him and spoil treatment unless she totally acquiesced to his insatiable demands for "love and intimacy."

The unwary therapist can get trapped into playing along with the anxious partner's excessive and unreasonable desires for emotional closeness and reassurance. These anxious individuals often present themselves as the healthy "victims" of their spouses' alleged "neurotic" detachment, lack of intimacy, inability to communicate, or overinvolvement in work.

While these are often real and serious issues in the treatment of couples with sexual panic disorder, intimacy and communication have become sacrosanct in our culture and the "accused" spouse and even the naive therapist often "buy" the anxious partner's erroneous assessment of the situation. The guilty "non-intimate" (normal) partner may not feel free to object and may think he should work on his "lack of intimacy." The unsophisticated therapist may agree to this inappropriate goal. But the real problem in these cases is the panicky partner's excessive desire for intimacy and her obsessive need for constant contact, communication, and overexpressiveness. These obsessive individuals alienate their spouses and drive them to distraction with their jealousies and their insatiable demands.

During the initial session with couples who present with false intimacy problems, I often raise a question as to which partner might have to change more extensively to improve the relationship. To the amazement and bitter disappointment of the anxious partner who had fully expected that the therapist would side with her in her quest for "greater intimacy," and to the vast relief of the one who had been labeled the "sick" one and who had feared that successful therapy would entail total emotional slavery for him, I might say:

> *(To the wife):* "I can see that you feel shut out and abandoned and that you *(to the husband)* feel very pressured. But I can't tell at this point if you *(to the wife)* are excessively needy or if you *(to the husband)* are abnormally detached or incapable of intimacy. We will need more information to figure that out."

Sometimes, when the phobic partner's emotional demands are clearly outrageous, I might be more direct:

> "I believe that your demands for attention and closeness and communication are excessive and would turn off any partner."

Case Vignette #15: Jane and John

An interchange of this kind took place when a middle-aged couple presented themselves with the complaint that the husband had avoided sex with his wife for the past 14 years. His wife was understandably distressed about this. He assumed full responsibility and felt guilty. John was a sensitive passive man; Jane was an anxious, obsessive-compulsive woman with an underlying panic disorder who virtually enslaved her husband. At her insistence, he came straight home from his office each day and spent every minute of his nonworking time with her. He had to accompany her to do the family shopping and all the other household errands which she saved up until he came home. He had to wash her hair. He had to listen to her recount every detail of her day each evening without interruption. If she did not have enough to tell him, she would insist on reading the newspaper to him. She demanded that he go to bed and rise at the same time that she did and she would have violent rages if he did not comply with any of her . requests. Not surprisingly, the husband had had no desire for sex for over a decade. He was chronically depressed and suffered from frequent and severe migraines.

At the close of the initial evaluation session, I told the wife that I understood how much she needed her husband and how painful it must be for her to be separated from him even for an hour, but that I thought her behavior was excessive and I feared that it might eventually drive her husband away. I could not in good conscience enter into a therapeutic contract to attempt to improve the husband's sexual response under the present circumstances, but I offered the wife the opportunity to explore ways in which she could become less demanding and more appealing to him so as to improve their marriage and their sex life. She was furious but accepted my offer. He was astounded.

The Avoidance of Commitment and Intimacy

Unlike the avoidance of sex which is an understandable reaction to real difficulties in a couple's relationship—for example, as a response to a partner's obsessive pressuring—patients with true intimacy and commitment conflicts frequently develop secondary sexual aversions to attractive partners who behave appropriately. In those cases the avoidance of sexual intimacy represents a defense against their deeper conflicts about love.

Good sex and emotional closeness heighten the vulnerabilities of individuals who are overly sensitive to separation and loss and interfere with their defensive avoidance. Such cases are among the most difficult and challenging to treat and require great persistence, creativity, and flexibility, as well as advanced skills in brief psychodynamic and conjoint therapy on the part of the therapist.

Their strong need for a close emotional relationship versus their vulnerability once they allow themselves to love predisposes individuals with panic disorder related separation and rejection problems to develop particularly tenacious and destructive commitment conflicts. These couples tend to show considerable resistance to treatment.

When the person whose intimacy fears have been heightened by the process of sex therapy resists, we first confront him with the defensive meaning of his sexual avoidance. If the relationship is basically sound, we attempt to get him to understand that his fears of being hurt by his lover are groundless and based on distortions derived from the past, and that his avoidance of closeness is a defense against his vulnerability to separation and rejection. If this does not work, we attempt to bypass his defenses with fantasy.

These patients' underlying fears of intimacy can occasionally be assuaged, by the therapist's clearly expressed position that his mate truly reciprocates his love (if this is true) and that his fears of being hurt are without substance or exaggerated. Even more persuasive that it is safe to open up is a change in the partner's behavior in the direction of greater sensitivity to and acceptance of his emotional needs and vulnerabilities. In these cases, working with the partner toward this end, it is a major objective of treatment, as was illustrated in the case of Norma, the "morning painter" (p. 127).

But long-standing fears of closeness seldom yield to realistic reassurances and the patient must be confronted with the self-destructive effects of his defensive detachment. But often, even the realization that eventually they destroy or escape from all intimate relationships and that they are likely to end up with lonely, empty lives does not suffice to break the therapeutic impasse. At this point, we move on to explore the deeper roots of the patient's problems in much greater detail and clarify the connections between his current difficulties and his childhood family experiences. When the patient has panic disorder, we carefully work through the deleterious effects that his vulnerability had on his psychosexual development and relate his current defensive avoidance of closeness to this. As long as the couple is benefitting from such insights and moving closer sexually, we usually do not use medication. But with couples who are "stuck" in treatment because the vulnerable partner cannot give up his defensive avoidance, medication can be very helpful in some cases.

It is also important to review the patient's prior romantic relationships because some individuals, especially those with overreactions to separations, have been badly hurt in the past and they cannot risk another commitment until this issue has been worked through in treatment.

Sexual Fantasy and Erotica

In more resistant couples the therapeutic explorations described above are supplemented by attempts to *bypass* the patient's sexual avoidance and his fears of commitment by means of fantasy and erotica.

Erotic fantasies, especially those with variant sexual themes, are regarded as pathological by many psychoanalysts. However, I think it makes more sense to view a person's erotic fantasies as constructive adaptations to sexual conflicts. Sexual fantasies can often be traced to a person's early childhood. They are the remnants of the child's primitive attempts to "bypass" the sexual anxieties that were generated by early masturbation guilt or forbidden incestuous wishes. For example, a child who has received harsh prohibition against masturbation might develop masochistic, erotic fantasies. In this manner, he manages to attain his sexual gratification while at the same time he expiates his guilt.

We conceptualize sexual fantasy and erotica as constructive adaptations to and a means of bypassing sexual inhibitions. As such, they have an important place in the treatment of sexual aversions and ISD.

The therapist's encouragement to use and to enjoy erotic fantasies and to share these with the partner legitimizes the patient's own old psychic strategies for "bridging" over his sexual conflicts and frees him to use these psychic devices in the service of his therapy.

An assignment that calls for an aversive patient to watch a videotape that depicts his favorite fantasy can distract him from the threatening awareness that he is making love to the woman with whom he fears intimacy and commitment. He can take refuge in imagery to circumvent his fears of closeness.

Sexual fantasy and erotica are sometimes useful "detours" to get around the sexual aversions of individuals who have a "madonna-whore" split between their erotic and intimate feelings. If the wife can accept this as her husband's problem and does not regard his lust for a fantasy "whore" as a personal rejection, erotic imagery and role-playing can be an effective tool for improving the couple's sexual relationship. She can gratify his sexual fantasy and "bypass" his "madonna" inhibition by playing the role of "whore" in the bedroom, but this only works if this is compatible with her own desires.

Erotic fantasy is also excellent for controlling performance anxiety which places an additional burden on men with sexual aversions when they try to make love without desire. Assignments that call for using erotica prior to sexual encounters can help put a patient in a mood for sex and serve as antidotes for the negative mental images or "antifantasies" that are often used to avoid sexual feelings by patients with ISD and sexual aversion disorders (Kaplan, 1979). Also, the intimate bond between a couple is strengthened when they can accept and share their fantasies openly. When each knows that nothing need be hidden from the other, they often become more comfortable and secure in the relationship. One of the goals of sex therapy is to help the patient learn to make himself comfortable in the sexual situation. "Tuning out" the partner with fantasy or erotica is sometimes an excellent strategy.

But some patients are too guilty about using erotica, and couch their objections on the grounds that this is "immoral" or "sick," or that the use of erotic imagery while with a partner is disloyal and constitutes "cheating."

In sex therapy we place a great deal of emphasis on freeing patients from sexual guilt and we encourage couples to accept and share each other's fantasies. We take the position that erotic imagery is no more immoral or deceitful than a soothing drink and that the use of fantasy is constructive as long as this increases a couple's sexual intimacy and pleasure together.

Resistance to erotic fantasy is sometimes mobilized by a misconception that is common among sexually guilty patients, that they must choose between their "dirty" fantasy and making "clean," affectionate, "normal" love to their spouse. The therapist's encouragement to use erotica in the context of the couple's lovemaking, her judgment that a couple's sharing fantasy is normal and constructive, and her efforts to work with the partner to get her to accept the patient's erotic fantasies—in short, the therapist's "permission" to have both—may be a relief for many.

Secure partners who are open sexually usually have no objections to their mate's use of fantasy. In fact, some welcome the relief from anxiety and the distraction from obsessive concerns with rejection and performance that erotica offer to their anxious partner, along with the additional pleasure this can bring to their own sexual experience. But the very independence created by the use of erotica which is so beneficial for the symptomatic patient can be extremely threatening to an insecure partner. Rejection sensitive wives are often jealous and threatened by their husband's excitement with fantasy—"I want him to be excited only with me." A partner's adamant resistance to erotica can be a major problem in the treatment of individuals who are able to function only with fantasy. The partner's loving sharing of his fantasy as an expression of her commitment to his sexual pleasure is the key to the successful outcome of many cases involving intimacy and commitment problems. The wife's unambivalent acceptance of her husband's desire and his need for erotica and her reassurance that this will not diminish him in her eyes are especially important for helping couples where the man is ashamed and guilty about his homosexual, transvestite, voyeuristic, or fetishistic desires.

Some of my most frustrating treatment failures can be directly attributed to my inability to work through the partner's resistance to accepting the mate's fantasy.

CHAPTER 7

Drugs and the
Psychodynamic Process:
Some Hypotheses
and Speculations

The following observations, conjectures, and hunches about drugs and dynamic therapy interactions have evolved from comparing the therapeutic process in patients with sexual panic disorders with and without medication over the past 15 years.*

This experience was extremely valuable for generating hypotheses but, until they are tested systematically with double-blind controlled studies, the ideas discussed in this chapter remain in the realm of speculation.

Although there have been a handful of reports by psychoanalysts suggesting that psychoactive drugs might potentiate the psychodynamic process under certain circumstances (Group for the Advancement of Psychiatry, 1975; Cooper, 1985), these observations run contrary to the deeply entrenched view of many psychodynamically minded clinicians that medication is contraindicated, or at least inadvisable, while psychoanalytic or psychodynamically oriented therapy is in progress. These objections are based on the erroneous premise that all psychoactive medications "cover up" the patient's anxiety and interfere with such crucial dynamic processes as the attainment of insight, conflict resolution, and "working through."

There is no doubt that exploratory psychotherapeutic work requires

---

* Most of our patients and couples with sexual dysfunctions and panic disorders were treated with psychodynamically oriented psychotherapy. Those who were not appropriate candidates for brief treatment were offered psychodynamically oriented long-term individual, group, or marital therapy. By 1980 we were including on a regular basis antipanic drugs in the treatment regimen of all patients with sexual dysfunctions who also had panic disorders.

that the patient develop a heightened awareness of his feelings of anxiety, anger, love, and sadness, and that he trace the development of these affects to their origins in early childhood.

Drugs that exert a depressant effect on the central nervous system (CNS) such as alcohol, hypnotics, narcotics, and tranquilizing and antianxiety agents could, in fact, be misused by patients to anesthetize themselves emotionally in the service of their resistance to analysis, especially when they are used in high doses. For these reasons, it is our practice to defer sex therapy with patients who are addicted to alcohol, narcotics, sedatives, and tranquilizers until they are abstinent and we seldom prescribe antianxiety drugs during the treatment process.

But a distinction must be made between such tranquilizing and sedative agents that depress the CNS and which could potentially be used to *avoid* the full impact of psychotherapy by resistant patients, and antipanic drugs which do the opposite. Antipanic drugs are *not* CNS *depressants*. They are *antidepressants*. These drugs have an analgesic effect on certain kinds of psychic pain, but they do not anesthetize a person's emotions nor cloud his conscious awareness, nor can they be used to avoid or resist the treatment process.

Our clinical experience also runs contrary to these theoretical objections. When we compare the treatment of medicated and unmedicated patients with underlying panic disorders, it becomes clear that these drugs do *not* impede the quality of the dynamic process. As a matter of fact, psychodynamic therapy often becomes *more productive* and treatment proceeds *more rapidly* after a patient is medicated.

Patients who are adequately medicated tend to produce more significant dreams, memories, and associations, and this material emerges earlier in treatment.

These drugs seem to make it possible for patients to face feelings and issues which had been intolerably painful in their unmedicated state.

Blocked and rigidly defended patients often become less resistant when they are confronted with their defenses. They can accept interpretations of sensitive unconscious material more easily after the drugs have diminished their excessive emotional vulnerabilities.

Orthopedic surgeons prescribe analgesics to diminish their patients' pain to enable them to exercise their injured and inflamed shoulder or hip while it is healing. Unless it is mobilized, the body part will "freeze" permanently into a locked and useless position regardless of how skillful the surgery.

By analogy, the protection the panic-blocking drugs can afford patients against their psychic pain can facilitate the attainment of insight and conflict resolution by helping to mobilize them to move away from their powerless and "frozen" positions in life.

We first noticed that the drugs seemed to enhance the psychodynamic process in brief sex therapy. But when we began to medicate patients with underlying panic states who were undergoing long-term reconstructive psychodynamic therapy for relationship difficulties, neurotic symptoms, and personality disorders, we noticed that in a number of cases patients who had been making exceedingly slow (or no) progress in their analyses or long-term psychodynamic therapies (with myself and other analysts) seemed to begin to move rapidly after they were medicated.

After looking closely at some of these cases, I have come to believe that a similar synergy between drugs and the psychodynamic process can also operate in long-term reconstructive psychodynamic treatment in certain cases.

The following case illustrates the kinds of observations which have raised this possibility.

Case Vignette #16: Gary

The patient was a 50-year-old author who had been in analysis for eight years for a number of long-standing neurotic and characterological problems. He had intense sexual anxiety and avoidance, premature ejaculation, recurrent periods of impotence, and occasional episodes of exhibitionism which troubled him greatly. He could not commit himself to a monogamous relationship, but he enjoyed an active social life and he considered himself "irresistible" to women.

Gary was a brilliant, sensitive man and in his analysis he had obtained valid insights into some of his neurotic problems and their childhood origins. However, despite his having gotten "in touch with" his infantile anger, and although he had catharted his violent rage against his father and vented his fury at his mother for years during his analysis, the patient was still apt to fly into a violent rage at the slightest sign of criticism or disrespect, and he continued to make life difficult for himself with his irresistible impulse to provoke "father figures."

Gary also remained ambivalent and frequently impotent with women. He attributed this to the anger he still bore towards his mother because he had acquired the "pseudo insight" in his analysis that she had been sexually attracted to him and had "led me on" when he was a boy. He "recalled" that she had once invited him into her bed when he was 11 and then expelled him abruptly when he had an erection.

The patient had a panic disorder with severe separation anxiety and hypersensitivity to rejection which had not been recognized in his prior treatment. He had a history of panic attacks and school phobia during childhood, and he frequently experienced panics in sexual situations. He was aware that he phobically avoided monogamous romantic attachments to protect himself from his vulnerabilities, as even a hint of rejection could "make me ill." He had been involved with a number of women, sometimes for years, but he had never lived with anyone and had never married.

The patient's sexual panics abated on 275 mgms. of Tofranil. He also became notably less sensitive to rejection.

Shortly after he had made impressive improvements in his sexual functioning, Gary angrily complained that I was trying to sabotage his relationship with his current girlfriend. He believed I was doing this because I was secretly in love with him and jealous of other women in his life.

I confronted the lack of substance of this transferential distortion and we explored its origins. He was finally able to face the exceedingly painful memories of rejection by his mother which had been covered up by the distortion that his mother desired him sexually.

It turned out that he had felt rejected by my obvious approval when he reported that sex with his girlfriend was now very good, just as he once was hurt when his mother asked the maid to give him his lunch. He had felt that if his mother really loved him she would not delegate the task of feeding him to a servant, and that if I really cared for him I would not delegate sexual tasks to his girlfriend. He had denied by reversing reality the painful truth that neither I nor his mother had a romantic interest in him.

He was finally able to own up to the humiliating fact that he had been a homely, skinny, nervous, awkward kid with thick glasses and a big nose. He had agonized over and repressed his fear that no female would ever want him, least of all his mother who was in reality deeply in love with the patient's father.

Gary's father had been a tall, extremely handsome, elegant, and successful man who had been very popular with women. Actually, the father had been rather generous with the boy. Gary's violent hatred grew out of his old unresolved envy and jealousy because his father was much more attractive and powerful than the patient ever hoped to be, and most of all because his mother had so obviously preferred her husband to Gary. The patient had protected himself from these unbearable realities by distorting his mother's attentions to him when her husband was absent into a fantasy that she was sexually attracted to him and secretly preferred him to his father. He came to grips with the sad reality that his mother had exploited his love. She had sought him out only when his father was away, when she would spend a good deal of time with him, mostly because of her own anxiety. But she would cruelly ignore the boy when her husband came home!

I have the sense that if the medication had not diminished his exquisite emotional hypersensitivity, the patient might have continued to resist these assaults on his defensive grandiosity. But in his less vulnerable medicated state, he was able to work through these and other sensitive issues and he began to make rapid progress in treatment.

The value of these drugs in long-term reconstructive therapy is seen most clearly when self-destructive patterns of avoidance paralyze the patient's functioning in significant areas and/or when separation anxiety related issues are central to his psychopathology.

Neurotic patients with underlying panic disorders are often highly resistant to reconstructive treatments and drugs can help in several ways. Some of these phobic individuals avoid significant areas of experience in their quest for a refuge from their panics, and they may end up with serious deficits in sex, love, and work. In these cases there is a realistic basis for the patient's rage, depression, and low self-esteem, and under such circumstances, it is difficult for the therapist to work effectively on these issues. But if the patient succeeds with the help of medication in mastering his phobic avoidance of sex or equally crippling avoidance of other vital functions, and he finds that he can now function sexually, or, have a relationship or get through medical school, just like everyone else, his resistance to insight and his needs for his old neurotic and characterological defenses may diminish. It is under such circumstances, and when the psychoanalgesic effects of the drugs are used in the service of reconstructive psychotherapy, that long-lasting and positive changes in the patient's personality structure become possible.

Initially, the idea that these drugs might prove useful in the treatment of personality disorders and long-standing difficulties with object relationships seemed foreign to me because I had been accustomed to thinking that structural personality changes could be brought about only by long-term psychodynamic therapeutic techniques. But on second thought, it is well known that the chronic abuse of marijuana and alcohol to escape from life's problems can have permanent deleterious effect on an individual's personality and family relationships. On the same theory, drugs which can be used to help a person *face* his difficulties might have a place in the treatment of long-standing personality disorders and marital problems.

Some of these positive drug-dynamic therapy interactions are clearly related to the patient's new freedom from panic attacks. But I would also speculate that another important element is the apparent ability of these substances to diminish the patient's pathological separation anxiety and his hypersensitivity to rejection and criticism."*

Separation anxiety and defenses against this often play a key role in the marital problems and interpersonal difficulties of patients with sexual panic states. Up to now we could treat this problem with only one of several psychological strategies. Psychodynamic therapies focus their efforts on exploring the early childhood roots of the person's separation problems. The objective of the behavioral approaches is to try to modify the individual's excessive anxiety about asserting himself with his current partner. Marital therapists deal with the pathological interactions that grow out of the panicky partner's hypersensitivity to separations and rejections by attempting to improve the couple's system of communication.

Theoretically, all these methods can eradicate the patient's pathological reactions to separations in persons with neurotic problems who are physiologically normal. But the best that psychological interventions have to offer individuals who have biological separation anxiety is to help them cope more constructively with their emotional hypersensitivity.

ANTIPANIC DRUGS AND SEPARATION ANXIETY

The efficacy of antipanic drugs for separation anxiety in children with school avoidance and separation problems has been well-documented (Gittelman-Klein, 1975b; Gittelman-Klein & Klein, 1980). But

---

* The term "rejection sensitivity" has been used by Klein and others to describe patients with "atypical depressions" (Quitkin et. al., 1984) who become seriously depressed when they are rejected by someone they love. The terms "rejection sensitivity" and "hypersensitivity" to rejection and criticism, are used here to mean only that the person overreacts to rejection and criticism from significant people in his life. We have frequently observed a constellation of *separation anxiety,* and *hypersensitivity* to *rejection* and *criticism* in patients with sexual panic states.

although there is a sound theoretical basis for predicting that these medications should also diminish the separation problems of adults with panic disorder, this has not yet been scientifically investigated.

We have seen obvious improvements in the clinical manifestations of excessive separation anxiety in a number of our patients with sexual panic states. It is my impression that this was, at least in some cases, related to medication. However it is clearly not possible to separate the effects of the insights and improvements in the couple's emotional and sexual relationships that were gained from the psychological aspects of therapy from the drug effects, without clinical studies that control these variables.

DRUGS AND THE PROCESS OF CONJOINT THERAPY

Separation Anxiety in Conjoint Treatment

Some marital therapists have expressed concern that psychoactive drugs might interfere with the process of working out basic, permanent improvements in the couple's pathological marital system. They fear that these substances will artificially obscure the fundamental causes of the couple's struggles, as alcohol does in the marriages of alcoholics, and make these inaccessible to therapeutic intervention.

However, our clinical experience does not support this view. When destructive marital interactions grow out of the couple's panic disorder related difficulties with separation, rejection, and criticism, the antipanic drugs can help them face their real problems, in some cases for the first time in their relationship. In couples who basically love one another, the psychoanalgesic effects of these drugs may diminish a partner's vulnerability to hurt sufficiently to allow latent intimate and loving feelings to emerge.

In the first place, these drugs can facilitate the process of sexual therapy. Couples with separation problems are often involved in recurrent crises that center around the vulnerable partner's touchiness. Any hint of rejection can send these individuals into rage and despair. Their insecurities may escalate to panic proportions during sex therapy, creating crises which are an obstacle to the treatment process. The process of sex therapy becomes much smoother when the anxious partner can be medicated successfully and when a small setback or misunderstanding no longer causes a major catastrophe.

At times, however, more fundamental systemic improvements in a couple's relationship seem to follow a reduction of the partner's separation anxiety when this has been a major element in their sexual difficulty.

Case Vignette #17: Grace and Gino

Grace is a tall, slim, attractive 39-year-old housewife of Irish Catholic extraction who had been married for 19 years to Gino, age 40, a well-dressed man, somewhat shorter than his wife. He is a successful restaurateur. His background is Italian-American. The couple have five children.

The couple wanted treatment for Grace's long-standing aversion to sex and her inability to experience sexual pleasure and orgasm.

Gino loved his beautiful wife with an obsessive intensity. He was extremely anxious and insecure about his sexual performance with Grace, but had no problems in casual relationships. He continually pressured Grace for sex because he felt even more insecure and anxious when they abstained. Not surprisingly, his anxious, compulsive performance-oriented approach to lovemaking created an unpleasantly tense ambiance and she tried to avoid sex to the extent that this was possible. When there was no escape, she passively endured the experience as best she could. The couple were seeking help at this time because of a crisis created by Grace's discovery that Gino had been having an affair with an actress. He had panicked and begged her not to leave him. She wanted to keep the family together and acknowledged that she had been partially at fault because she had not been satisfying her husband sexually.

Grace grew up in a warm, happy family and enjoyed excellent, close relationships with her parents and six siblings. Strict moral values were stressed in the home, parochial schools and Catholic college which she and her sisters attended. Grace had had virtually no sexual experience prior to her marriage to Gino.

Sexual intercourse had been physically painful for Grace through-out the first years of their marriage until the delivery of their first child (presumably because of vaginismus). The combination of her sexually restrictive upbringing and the painful sex, together with her husband's sexual anxiety and their inadequate lovemaking techniques, had all contributed to the sexual problems of this otherwise emotionally healthy woman.

The husband phobically avoided heights, large dogs, and deep water. He tended to be hypochondriacal. He denied spontaneous panics, but his anxiety level was high. When he tried to exercise, he would become faint and breathless and his pulse would race. His mother had been agoraphobic for many years. Gino was not an open, intimate person, but he had developed good social skills and enjoyed considerable popularity. His intelligence, together with his driving, compulsive work habits, had enabled him to achieve impressive business success.

Apart from their sexual problem, the couple enjoyed a harmonious relationship and there were numerous positive elements in this marriage.

Gino had literally fallen in love with Grace at first sight and remains obsessively in love with her today. She is more ambivalent, but she appreciates his generosity and his devotion to her and to their children.

I initially saw Grace by herself for her sexual inhibition, which had been an important element in the couple's problem. She became orgastic on self-stimulation after a brief course of psychosexual therapy. I then attempted to include Gino, to work on his sexual anxiety. However, the process of treatment threatened the defenses he had built up against his overwhelming anxiety. He felt exposed and vulnerable in the conjoint sessions and he misinterpreted my assignments as implying that he was lacking as a lover. He insisted that he had never had problems with other women and that the fault lay entirely with Grace's traditional Catholic upbringing.

I tried to "bypass" Gino's resistance to revealing his inner feelings to his wife by suggesting that he work individually with another therapist in our group. But he left treatment after three sessions.

Grace consulted me again two years later. She had had a sexually gratifying affair with a young artist. However, sex with Gino had become even more unpleasant for her. She now knew that she had the capacity to enjoy sexual intimacy with a man and she wanted to improve the sexual relationship with her husband. He seemed to sense and be threatened by her increasing sexual openness and had become even more obsessive and compulsive in his lovemaking. He was lately beginning to have problems maintaining his erections. Gino was now more afraid of losing his potency and his wife than of facing therapy, and he was ready to commit himself to treatment.

The panicky husband's obsessive pressuring, his sexual anxiety, and his compulsive performance-oriented lovemaking were now the only immediate obstacle to this couple's sexual improvement, and treatment focused on these issues.

The couple was locked into a vicious cycle. She was repelled by his sexual insecurities. Her failure to respond to him heightened his performance anxiety, and in turn she found his growing anxiety in bed increasingly difficult to tolerate.

Even before Gino's anxiety had diminished, their marriage had improved considerably through their work in conjoint therapy. They both gained a realistic understanding of the problems created by Gino's anxiety disorder for both of them, and they learned to handle this much more constructively. They became more open with one another and much of the anger went out of their relationship. Grace became more supportive and Gino's sexual functioning improved.

But all this did not eradicate the stab of anguish he felt whenever he sensed he was failing her as a lover, nor the moment of aversion she still had to fight within herself when he approached her bed. Despite their insights and their improved communications, he remained anxious about sex with his wife and she continued to feel repelled by her husband's sexual insecurity.

After Gino was medicated (alprazolam, 2 mgs, at bedtime for at least three weeks), he simply no longer experienced the familiar pang of panic as he approached Grace. For the first time in their relationship, he was free of his obsession about pleasing her. Less apprehensive about his performance, he could finally let himself fully enjoy making love to Grace, the woman who had always been his sexual fantasy, and she began to respond to his sexual energy.

Individuals who are afflicted with a biological vulnerability to separations do not experience feelings of love without concomitantly feeling afraid. Throughout their development from the time they were infants, their attachments have always coincided with the fear of losing the person they love or being hurt by that person. These individuals tend to incorporate their separation anxiety and their defenses against their vulnerability into all their subsequent romantic relationships. But these same protective mechanisms also create a barrier against the closeness and intimacy which they need so badly and this creates a dilemma for these sensitive persons.

If a medication had the capability to free them even in part from these encumbrances to love, patients with panic-disorder-related separation anxiety problems would become more open to conjoint therapy. When rejection and criticism lose the power to hurt them so deeply, it will be easier for them to give up their defenses against love and commitment. These drug-induced psychophysiologic changes can potentially be used in the context of marital therapy to encourage the couple to relate to each other in a more mature, open, mutually supportive, and loving manner, opening up the possibility of reversing the downward spiral of their interactions towards an upward direction.

DRUGS AND RECONSTRUCTIVE TREATMENTS

In sum, our experience with the patients and couples whom we have treated for sexual panic states raises the possibility that the "psychoanalgesic" effects of antipanic medications against the pain of rejection and loss and their ability to raise the panic threshold in these patients could enhance the long-term objectives of psychodynamic and conjoint marital therapy.

If this theory should prove valid, the therapeutic potential of these agents for patients with drug-responsive anxiety states could be much broader than merely facilitating the modification of specific phobic symptoms, such as the phobic avoidance of sex, and extend to increasing the patient's responsiveness to and the effectiveness of psychodynamic reconstructive therapies for complex personality, neurotic, and marital disorders.

These remarks should not be taken to imply that I am suggesting that psychotropic medication will ever make short shrift of dynamic therapy or that complex human problems will now be easy to treat. Unfortunately, even if the efficacy of these drugs for diminishing residual separation anxiety in adults becomes a proven fact, that will not be the case. At best, only a small proportion of psychiatric and sex therapy patients have drug-responsive panic disorders with separation problems. Also even when they are good responders, patients with underlying phobic anxiety syndrome who developed complex personality disorders and difficulties in their relationships will always require sensitive, insightful, dedicated therapeutic work. But even with very lengthy therapy, it is often difficult to help these patients in a definitive way. The astute use of medication by psychodynamically oriented therapists who also understand the part played by the biological elements of panic disorder in their patient's psychopathology promises to represent a real and significant improvement in the treatment of these complex disorders.

But I also do not want to convey the impression that psychoactive medications should be regarded as mere adjuvants to the psychotherapies. These drugs are clearly powerful therapeutic change agents in their own right. They are of proven benefit to patients with panic disorders who are not amenable to psychological treatments alone or who would receive only limited help from them.

What I am suggesting, however, is that these drugs also have a considerable and untapped therapeutic potential for the more complex psychological and marital problems of patients with panic disorders when they are used in a psychodynamic context and within a systems model of conjoint therapy.

Bibliography

Alzate, H., and Londono, M.L. Vaginal erotic sensitivity. *Journal of Sex and Marital Therapy, 10*(1), 1984.

American Psychiatric Association. *Diagnostic and Statistical Manual of Mental Disorders,* Third Edition. American Psychiatric Association: Washington, D.C., 1980.

American Psychiatric Association. *DSM-III-R in Development.* Second draft. Washington, D.C.: American Psychiatric Association, 1986.

Barbach, A.J. The experimental foundation of some new psychotherapeutic methods. In A.J. Barbach (Ed.) *Experimental Foundations of Clinical Psychology.* New York: Basic Books, 1962.

Birch, H.G., and Bitterman, M.E. Reinforcement and learning: The process of sensory integration. *Psychol. Rev., 56,* 367–383, 1949.

Bowlby, J. *Attachment and Loss. Vol. II Separation Anxiety and Anger.* New York: Basic Books, 1973.

Brady, J.P., Levitt, E.E., and Baydan, N. An operant reinforcement paradigm in the study of drug effects. *Dis. Nervous System, 23,* 1962.

Cavenar, Jr., J.P., and Michels, R. (Eds.). The psychosexual dysfunction. In *Psychiatry.* New York: 1985.

Cooper, A.M. Will neurobiology influence analysis? *American Journal of Psychiatry, 142*(12), 1985.

Crenshaw, T. The sexual aversion syndrome. *Journal of Sex and Marital Therapy, 11*(4), 1985.

Dollard, J., and Miller N.F. *Personality and Psychotherapy.* New York: McGraw Hill, 1950.

Erikson, E.H. *Identity Youth and Crisis.* New York: Norton, 1968.

Freud, S. Analysis of a phobia in five-year old boy. (Vol. x). *The Collected Works of Sigmund Freud.* London: Hogarth Press, 1966.

Friedman, M. *Overcoming the Fear of Success.* New York: Warner, 1981.

Gittelman, R., and Klein, D.F. Childhood separation anxiety and adult agoraphobia. In A.H. Tuma & J.D. Maser (Eds.) *Anxiety and the Anxiety Disorders.* Hillsdale, N.J.: Lawrence Erlbaum, 1985.

Gittelman-Klein, R., Psychiatric characteristics of the relatives of school phobic children. In S. Sankar (Ed.), *Mental Health in Children,* Vol. 1. New York: PJD Publications Ltd., 1975a.

Gittelman-Klein, R. Pharmacotherapy and management of pathological separation anxiety. *In Recent Advances in Child Psychopharmacology.* New York: Human Sciences Press, 1975b.

Gittelman-Klein, R., and Klein, D.F. Separation anxiety in school refusal and its treatment with drugs. In L. Herson & I. Berg (Eds.), *Out of School.* New York: John Wiley and Sons, 1980.

Gittelman-Klein, R., and Klein, D.F. School phobia: Diagnostic considerations in the light of imipramine effects. *Journal of Nervous and Mental Disorders, 156,* 1975.

Gorman, J.M., Fyer A.F., Glikich, J., King, D., and Klein, D.F. Effect of imipramine on prolapsed mitral valves of patients with panic disorder. *American Journal of Psychiatry, 138* (7), July 1981a.

Gorman, J.M., Fyer A.F., Glikich, J., King, D., and Klein, D.F. Effect of sodium lactate on patients with panic disorder and mitral valve prolapse. *American Journal of Psychiatry, 138* (2), February 1981b.

Group for the Advancement of Psychiatry. *Pharmacotherapy and Psychotherapy.* Report 93. New York: Mental Health Materials Center, 1975.

Jones, M.C. The elimination of children's fears. *Journal of Experimental Psychology,* 1924.

Kaplan, H.S. Ph.D. Thesis: The effects of alcohol on fear extinction. *Dissertation Abstracts, 16* (3), 1956.

Kaplan, H.S. *The New Sex Therapy.* New York: Brunner/Mazel, 1974.

Kaplan, H.S. Hypoactive sexual desire. *Journal of Sex and Marital Therapy, 3* (1), Spring 1977.

Kaplan, H.S. *Disorders of Sexual Desire.* New York: Brunner/Mazel, 1979.

Kaplan, H.S. *The Evaluation of Sexual Disorders: Psychological and Medical Aspects.* New York: Brunner/Mazel, 1983.

Kaplan, H.S., Fyer, A.J., and Novick, A. The treatment of sexual phobias: The combined use of anti-panic medication and sex therapy. *Journal of Sex and Marital Therapy, 8* (1), Spring 1982.

Kernberg, O.F. Early ego integration and object relations. *Annual New York Academy of Science.* New York: New York Academy of Science, 1972.

Kinsey, A.C., Pomeroy, W.B., and Martin, C.E. *Sexual Behavior in the Human Male.* Philadelphia: Saunders, 1948.

Kinsey, A.C., Pomeroy, W.B., Martin, C.E., and Gebhard, P.H. *Sexual Behavior in the Human Female.* Philadelphia: Saunders, 1953.

Klein, D.F. Delineation of two drug-responsive anxiety syndromes. *Psychopharmotherapy, 5,* 397–408, 1964.

Klein, D.F. Anxiety reconceptualized. In D.F. Klein & J.G. Rabkin (Eds.), *Anxiety: New Research and Changing Concepts.* New York: Raven Press, 1980a.

Klein, D.F., Gittelman-Klein, R., Quitkin, F., and Rifkin, A. *Diagnosis and Drug Treatment of Psychiatric Disorder.* Baltimore: Williams and Wilkins, 1980b.

Kohl, R. Adverse reactions to the rapid treatment of sexual problems. *Psychosomatics, 13*, (3), 185–190, May-June, 1972.

Leibowitz, M.R., and Klein, D.F. Treatment and assessment of phobic anxiety. *Journal of Clinical Psychology, 40,*1979.

Leibowitz, M.R., Quitkin, F.M., Stewart, J.W., McGrath, P.J., Harrison, W., Rabkin, J., Tricano, E., Markowitz, J.S., and Klein, D.F. Phenelzine vs. Imipramine in atypical depression. A preliminary report. *Archives of General Psychiatry, 120,* July 1984.

Lief, H.F. What's new in sex research? Inhibited sexual desire. *Medical Aspects of Human Sexuality, 11* (7), 1977.

LoPiccolo, L. Low libido states. Presented at the meeting of the American Association of Sex Therapists, Philadelphia, 1979.

Marks, I.M. *Living with Fear.* New York: McGraw-Hill, 1978.

Marks, I. Behavior therapy plus drugs in anxiety syndromes. In D.F. Klein & J.G. Rabkin (Eds.), *Anxiety: New Research and Changing Concepts.* New York: Raven Press, 1980.

Masters, W.H., and Johnson, V. *The Human Sexual Response.* Boston: Little, Brown, 1966.

Masters, W.H., and Johnson V. *Human Sexual Inadequacy.* Boston: Little, Brown, 1970.

Masters, W.H., and Johnson, V. *Homosexuality in Perspective.* Boston: Little, Brown, 1979.

Mavissakalian, M., and Michelson, L. Two-year follow-up study of exposure and Imipramine treatment of agoraphobia. *American Journal of Psychiatry, 143*(9), 1986.

Melman, A., Henry, D.P., Felten, D.P., and O'Connor, B. Effect of diabetes upon penile nerves in impotent patients. *Southern Medical Journal, 73,* 1980.

Mowrer, O.H. On the dual nature of learning: A reinterpretation of "conditioning" and "problem solving." *Harvard Education Review, 17,* 1974.

Mowrer, O.H. A stimulus-response analysis of anxiety and its role as a reinforcing agent. *Harvard Educational Review, 46,* 1939.

Mowrer, O.H., *Learning Theory and Personality Dynamics.* New York: Ronald Press, 1950.

Myers, R.M., Anxiety, neurosis and phobic states: Diagnosis and management. *British Medical Journal, 1,* 559–562, 1969.

Pitts, F.N., and McClune, J.N., Lactate metabolism in anxiety neurosis, *New England Journal of Medicine,* Dec. 21, 1967.

Quitkin, F.M., Harrison, W., Leibowitz, M., McGrath, P., Rabkin, J.G., Stewart, J., and Markowitz, J. Defining the boundaries of atypical depression. *Journal of Clinical Psychiatry, 45,* (7), (Sec. 2), July, 1984.

Quitkin, F.M., Schwartz, D., Leibowitz, M.R., Stewart, J.R., McGrath, P.J., Harris, W., Halpern, F., Puig-Antich, K., Triciano, E., Sachar, E.J., and Klein, D.F. Atypical depressives: A preliminary report of antidepressant response, sleep patterns and cortisol secretion. In P.J. Clayton & J.F. Barret (Eds.), *Treatment of Depression: Old Controversies and New Approaches.* New York: Raven Press, 1983.

Rickels, K., et al. Previous medication, duration of illness and placebo response. *Journal of Nervous and Mental Disease, 142,* 548–554, 1966.

Roth, M., and Meyers, D.H. Anxiety neurosis and phobic states: Diagnosis and management. *British Medical Journal, 1,* 1969.

Sager, C.J., Kaplan, H.S., Gundlach, R.H., Kremer, M., Lenz, R., and Royce, J.R., The marriage contract. In C.J. Sager & H.S. Kaplan (Eds.), *Progress in Group and Family Therapy.* New York: Brunner/Mazel, 1972.

Sargant, W., and Slater, E. *An Introduction to Physical Methods of Treatment in Psychiatry.* Baltimore: Williams & Wilkins, 1948.

Schover, L.R., and LoPiccolo, J. Treatment effectiveness for dysfunctions of sexual desire. *Journal of Sex and Marital Therapy, 8,* (3), 1982.

Scott, J.P., Stewart, J.M., and Dechelt, V.J. Separation in infant dogs: Emotional response and motivational consequence. *Separation and Depression: Clinical and Research Aspects.* Washington, D.C.: American Association for the Advancement of Science, 1973.

Sheehan, D.V., Ballenger, J., and Jacobson, G. Treatment of endogenous anxiety with phobic hysterical and hypochondriacal symptoms: *Archives of General Psychiatry, 37,* 1980.

Skinner, B.F. *The Behavior of Organisms: An Experimental Analysis.* New York: Appleton Century Crofts, 1938.

Skinner, B.F. *Science and Human Behavior.* New York: Macmillan, 1953.

Thomas, A., and Chess, S., *Temperament and Development.* New York: Brunner/Mazel, 1977.

Watson, J.B., and Rayner, R. Conditioned emotional reactions. *Journal Exp. Psychology, 3,* 1-14, 1920.

Weissman, M.M., Leckman, J.F., Merikangas, K.R., Gammon, G.D., and Prosoff, B.A. Depression and anxiety disorders in parents and children: Results from the Yale Family Study. *Archives of General Psychiatry, 41,* Sept. 1984.

Witkin, M.H. Sex therapy and penectomy. *Journal of Sex and Marital Therapy, 8*(3), 1982.

Wolpe, J. *Psychotherapy by Reciprocal Inhibition.* Palo Alto: Stanford University Press, 1958.

Zitrin, C.M., Klein, D.F., and Woerner, M.G. Behavior therapy, supportive therapy, imipramine and phobias. *Archives of General Psychiatry, 35,* 307-316, 1978.

Index

Abandonment, fear of, 106–107. *See also* Separation anxiety
Adjustment disorder, and anxiety, 69–70
Adolescence, sexual development in, 40, 90
Agitation, 75–76
Agoraphobia, 26, 45, 72, 86, 89
Alcohol, 73, 85
Alprazolam (Xanax), 7, 43, 73, 79, 86–87, 148
Alzate, H., 60n
Ambivalence, in relationships, 62–65
American Psychiatric Association, 3, 10, 25, 28, 69
Amitriptyline (Elavil), 78, 86
Anal period, 58–59
Anorgasmia, 35
  medication and, 77–79
Anxiety, 7, 45, 68, 98
  and agitation, 75–76
  anticipatory, 15, 71, 76
  chronic, 71, 73
  generalized, 70
  new biological theory of, 43–50, 56–61
  reactive, 69, 74
  phobic, 6, 30–34, 48–49
  sexual difficulties and, 69–70
  syndromes of, 69–77
Avoidance, sexual. *See* Sexual avoidance
Avoidance patterns, 3, 15–16, 29–33, 39, 72, 143

Barbiturates, 26, 73, 80, 85
Behavioral theory
  of phobic states, 37–40
  and sex therapy, 7, 47, 49–50, 85, 93–94, 103–107

and theory of anxiety, 49–50
Behaviorism, and theory of anxiety, 49–50
Benzodiazepines, 70, 71, 73, 77, 79, 80
Beta blockers, 77, 88
Birch, H. G., 97
Bitterman, M. F., 97
Bowlby, J., 44n
Brady, J. P., 85
"Bridging," 114. *See also* "Bypassing"
"Bypassing," 113, 126, 127, 136, 147

Castration, fear of, 41
Chess, S., 48
Chlordiazepoxide, 75
Chlormipramine, 74
Clitoral eroticism, 35, 60n. *See also* Orgasm
Closeness, unreasonable desire for, 133–134
Commitment
  avoidance of, 135–136
  fear of, 65
Conditioning theory, 38–39, 85
Confrontation, 17, 119, 120
  progressive, 114–115, 119
Constructive realism, anxiety and, 33–34
Contractual disappointments, 64
Cooper, A. M., 139
Crenshaw, T., 3, 17
Crises, therapeutically controlled, 105
Cultural conditioning, role in sexual panic states, 105

Defense mechanisms, 42
Denial, 17, 18, 32
Depersonalization disorder, 74

155

Depression, 18, 68, 73, 75-76
  agitated, 73
  "atypical," 34n
Desensitization, 6, 31, 85, 87, 94n, 97,
  98-99, 101-102
  in vivo, 37, 86, 94
Desimipramine (Norpramine), 86
Desmethylimipramine (Norpramin), 78
Diagnosis, 25
  differential, 68, 69
  See also DSM-III
Diazepam, 71, 75, 80
Differential diagnosis, 68, 69
Diuretics, 78
Dollard, J., 38
Drugs. *See* Medication(s)
DSM-III (1980), 3, 10, 25, 26-27, 28,
  60n, 69
DSM-III-R, 3, 10

Erectile dysfunction, 88
Erikson, E. H., 57-58
Erotica, 136-138
Extinction, 39, 98-99

Fantasies
  erotic, 96, 136-138
  incestuous, 117-118
Fear-alarm response, 45-46
"Flooding," 97n
Freud, S., 40-41, 57, 60n
Fyer, Abby, 77

Gender specific problems, 54
Gittelman-Klein, R., 29-30, 44, 144
Gorman, J.M., *et al.*, 25n, 26n
Group for the Advancement of
  Psychiatry, 139
Guilt, cultural, 121-124

Helplessness, fear of, 25
Hypochondriasis, 73, 75

Identification, with therapist, 122
Imipramine (Tofranil), 5, 29, 81, 86,
  88-89, 90, 142
Impotence, 95. *See also* Erectile
  dysfunction
Incest, 105
Incestuous fantasies, 117-118
Insight, 16-17
Intercourse, 95
  prohibiting, 70
Intimacy
  avoidance of, 126, 135-136
  excessive desire for, 133-134

fear of, 65, 135-136
In vivo desensitization, 37, 86, 94
ISD (inhibited sexual desire), 11, 20-21,
  36, 66

Johnson, V., 50, 62, 66, 70, 94, 99
Jones, M. C., 37

Kaplan, H. S., 66, 67, 84n, 85, 97, 98,
  105, 110n, 114, 137
  et al. (1982), 4n
Kinsey, A. C., *et al.*, 52
Klein, D. F., 4, 6, 27, 29-30, 34, 43,
  144
  et al., 87

Learning theory, and phobic states,
  37-40, 49-50
LoPiccolo, J., 11
Liebowitz, M. R., 34n, 77
Loss of control, fear of, 25

McClune, J. N., 25n
MAO B inhibitor (Deprenyl), 79
MAOI (monoamine inhibiting)
  medications, 4, 7, 34n, 43, 73, 76,
  77-79, 82, 86-87. *See also*
  Medication(s), antidepressant
Marks, I. M., 94
Masters, W. H., 50, 62, 66, 70, 94, 99
Masturbation, 52, 96, 105
Medication(s), 3-4, 5-9, 28-29, 68-83,
  86-93, 97-98, 139-150
  antianxiety, 70, 71, 73, 83
  antidepressant, 4, 7, 43, 44, 73, 76,
  77-79, 139n, 140
  antipanic, 3-4, 6, 9, 24, 81, 84, 85,
  86, 89, 140-150
  depressant, 140
  dosing strategy, 79-82, 85-86
  maintenance levels, 83
  placebo, 70
  pregnancy and, 101n
  and reconstructive treatments, 141,
  143, 149-150
  sexual side effects of, 68, 77-82,
  86-87, 88
Methamphetamine, 74
Meyers, D. H., 43
Miller, N. F., 38
Mitral valve prolapse, 26n, 29, 53
Modeling, therapist, 118, 122
Mowrer, O. H., 38

New York State Psychiatric Institute
  Anxiety Clinic, 77

Nortryptyline (Aventil), 86

Obsessive-compulsive disorder, 73-74
Oedipal period, 40, 41, 59-61, 119
Oral period, 57-58
Orgasm, 11, 67, 96
  effect of medication on, 77-79
  prohibiting, 96
  vaginal, 60
Orthodox Judaism, sexual morality in,
  50, 51, 52, 105
Overprotection, parental, 31-33

Panic disorder syndrome, 4-5, 24-29,
  70, 73, 125-126
  atypical, 21-22, 27-28
  constructive adaptation to, 29, 33-34
  criteria for, 25-27
  and psychosexual dysfunction, 66-67
  with secondary phobia, 71-73
  and separation anxiety, 44-47
  sexual (*see* Sexual panic disorder)
  subclinical, 28
Parents
  constructive realism in, 33-34
  overidentification and
    overinvolvement by, 33
  overprotective, 31-33
  rejecting, 30-31
Partner engagement, 132-138
Pavlov, I., 38
Payne Whitney Clinic, New York
  Hospital-Cornell Medical Center, 4
  Human Sexuality Clinic, 8
Penetration, phobic avoidance of, 42,
  101-102
Performance anxiety, 24, 35-36, 50, 54,
  95, 115
Phobia(s), 70-73
  sexual (*see* Sexual phobias)
  social, 76-77
Phobic anxiety syndrome, 6, 43, 46, 50.
  See also Panic disorder syndrome
Phobic states
  extinction of, 93-107
  learning theory (or behavioral)
    concept of, 37-40, 49-50
  new biological (or integrated) theory
    of, 43-47, 56-61
  partial, 100-101
  psychodynamic concept of, 40-43,
    56-61
  secondary, 71-73
  simple, 70-71
  specific stimulus, 103-104
Pitts, F. N., 25n

Placebos, 70
Power struggles, marital, 63
Premature ejaculation, 12, 70
Priapism, 78
Psychoanalytic theory, 57-61, 113
  and phobic states, 40-43
Psychodynamic theory, and phobic
  states, 40-43, 56-61, 103
Psychopharmacology, 7, 68-83. *See also*
  Medication(s)
Psychotherapy
  behavioral, 7 (*see also* Sex therapy,
    behaviorally oriented)
  directive-supportive, 33
  psychodynamic, 6-8, 40-43, 56-61,
    103
  reconstructive, 141, 143, 149-150
  See also Sex therapy

Quitkin, F. M., *et al.*, 34n, 144n

Rationalization, 17, 18
Rayner, R., 37
Reciprocal inhibition, 37
Reinforcement theory, 38, 39
Rejection
  oversensitivity to, 31, 34n, 36, 66, 76,
    106, 107
  parental, 30-31
"Rejection sensitivity," 34n, 144n
Relationship problems, 62-65, 125-138
Resistance(s), 32, 107-110, 114, 117,
  119, 126, 147
  to erotic fantasy, 138
  joining, 119
  and sexual guilt, 121
Rickels, K., 70
Roman Catholicism, sexual morality in,
  50-51, 105
Roth, M., 43

Sager, C. J., *et al.*, 64
Sargant, W., 74
Schover, L. R., 11
Scott, J. P., *et al.*, 44
Self-disclosure, therapist, 123-124
Sensate Focus (SF) exercises, 94-97, 99,
  102-103, 116, 120, 127-128
Separation anxiety, 21, 28, 34-36, 44n,
  72, 90, 106, 111-112, 125-126, 133
  antipanic drugs and, 144-145
  in conjoint treatment, 145-149
  and panic disorder, 44-47, 86
  parental overprotection and, 31-33
  parental rejection and, 30-31

Sex therapy
  behaviorally oriented, 7, 47
  brief dynamic, 56, 85, 113, 126, 141
  conjoint, 62, 104, 126-138, 145-149
  couple as cotherapists in, 92-93
  emotional impact of, 104-107
  engaging couple in, 91, 132-138
  integrated approach to, 7, 47-49,
    84-124
  medication and, 5-9, 68-83 *passim*,
    86-93
  motivation for, 91
  psychodynamically oriented, 4, 6-8,
    47, 84, 103, 105-106, 111, 114-115,
    144
  resistance to, 32, 107-110, 117, 119,
    121, 126, 147
"Sexual anorexia," 11
Sexual aversion, 3, 4-5, 11, 14-15,
    24-29, 36, 84-85
  defined, 10
  partial, 99-100
  of partner, 35-36, 132-134
  primary and secondary, 17-18, 21, 56
  See also Sexual avoidance
Sexual avoidance, 3, 10-13, 19-20
  bilateral, 126
  patterns of, 15-16
  primary and secondary, 12, 24, 62
  See also Sexual aversion
Sexual conflicts, neurotic, 111-112
Sexual desire, hypoactive, 11. *See also*
    ISD
Sexual development, 40, 96-97
  preintercourse phases, 13-14
  psychosexual development, 40-43,
    57-61, 111
Sexual dysfunctions, panic disorders
    and, 66-67
Sexual panic disorder, 3, 10, 12, 14,
    18-19
  couple with, 62-65, 125-128

cultural conditioning and, 50-56, 105
etiology of, 50-56
relationship problems and, 62-65
See also Panic disorder syndrome
Sexual phobias, 11-15
  defined, 10-11
  intensity of, 14-15
  learning theory and, 39-40
  partial, 99-100
  primary and secondary, 17, 21
  psychodynamic theory and, 42-43
  types of, 13
Sheehan, D. V., *et al.*, 43
Skinner, B. F., 38, 39
Sodium lactate, 25n
Somatic symptoms, 16, 72-73, 75
Support, in therapeutic relationship, 70,
    114, 120-121, 126
Sympatholytic agents, 78

TCAs (tricyclic antidepressants), 4, 5, 7,
    25n, 34n, 43, 73, 76, 78-79, 86-87.
    See also Medication(s),
    antidepressant
Thomas, A., 48
Tofranil (Imipramine), 29, 86, 88-89,
    90, 142
Transference, 91, 102
  childhood, 64-65
Trazodone (Desyrel), 78
Treatment impasse, resolving, 119
Two-factor theory, 38

Urecholine, 78

Watson, J., 37
Weissman, M. M., *et al.*, 29, 44
Witkin, M. H., 105, 117
Wolpe, J., 94n

Zitrin, C. M., *et al.*, 43